MOTHERING ADDICTION

MOTHERING ADDICTION

BY LYNDA HARRISON HATCHER

"This intimate, raw and honest story is for everyone who has loved their child unconditionally. I found myself locked into the words on the pages, laughing, crying and mouth agape at times. Lynda Harrison Hatcher has willingly opened her heart and no doubt, this story will touch yours."

—— *Carol Vig, Beta Reader*

"Parents play an essential role in helping their child survive an addiction crisis. Their actions can literally mean the difference between life and death. Having worked with numerous families over the past 30 years navigate these treacherous waters with their children, I recommend *Mothering Addiction* without reservation. I have not found anyone who has articulated this subject matter in as personal and compelling a way as Lynda Harrison Hatcher."

— *Ann Hayes, President, Investigative Management Group*

★ **FRONTIER**PRESS

MOTHERING

ADDICTION

a memoir

LYNDA HARRISON HATCHER

✳ **FRONTIER**PRESS

For Sam, Charlotte, and Stuart

All of my life, I've been searching
For the words to say how I feel.
I'd spend my time thinking too much
And leave too little to say what I mean
I've tried to understand the best I can
All of my life.

All of My Life by Phil Collins

FOREWORD
Constance Costas

When Lynda Harrison Hatcher, a two-finger typist, decided to write a book, she didn't let any obstacles get in the way. Lynda has produced a brutally honest story laced with wisdom and humor. I am proud to have contributed. But let's be clear — Lynda made it happen — 100%.

She started with stories. She'd talk in streams of consciousness and I'd capture every word on my computer, asking questions, directing the flow. I began to see my own story in hers. Like Lynda, I'd wrung my hands over a son. I'd felt the shame and blame, lived the turmoil of substance abuse, feeling bewildered and helpless. I'd walked in her shoes. And, I happened to know, there were thousands of women like us, who'd found — or would find — themselves in the same boat. This is more than a story about Lynda and her son "Sam." She touches a nerve that few mothers are willing to admit even exists.

Lynda's story is unvarnished, occasionally unflattering, and always real. She and the women of *The Book Club* offer this reassurance to mothers: *You're not the only one. You're not alone.*

I knew Lynda had succeeded when my 80-year-old mother looked up after reading several chapters and said, "It's about me." After ten years of caring for my father before his death, she recognized the urgency of saving yourself from drowning when the strain of caring for someone you love is threatening to pull you under.

If you're wringing your hands over a child, this book is for you. And if you recognize a friend in this story, it's a book you will want to press into their hands. In Lynda's story, you will see yourself, you will meet kindred spirits, you will find wise counsel, free from judgement and, instead of drowning, you will find water wings to sustain you — until you can swim on your own.

———

Constance Costas is a writer and editor based in Richmond, Virginia.

INTRODUCTION

I n January of 1986, I held my first child, Sam, and cried grateful tears. Like so many women before me, I marveled at the sacred task of motherhood.

Twenty-something years later, when heroin tightened its grip on my son, I turned to church basement meetings and closed-door therapy sessions. But I found true solace when, one-by-one, women just like me stepped from the shadows to acknowledge their own private pain. We formed an underground alliance, codename: *The Book Club.* Together, we *mothered* addiction. With humor and humility, we navigated the knife-edged paradox of loving while letting go.

When I scanned bookstore shelves for a mother's story of parenting an addict-child, I came up short. I asked Bill Maher, an addiction specialist, why so few mothers wrote books about their experience. He answered with one word: Shame.

Some friends have debated the wisdom of publishing my dirty laundry. And more than a hundred times, I almost lost my nerve. But I wrote this book for the invisible casualties of addiction—the parents caught in the epidemic of youth substance abuse. With 26 million addicts in the U.S., there are 52 million mothers and fathers walking this desperate journey. I feel called to puncture the blame and shame that surrounds them. So yes, if that's what it takes, I'll string my dirty laundry on a clothesline from here to California. Like them, our family did the best we could under impossible circumstances. We made mistakes. We muddled through.

The events in this book took place between 1986 and 2016. I've told my story as honestly as I know how. But for the sake of my family and friends, I have changed names and reassigned scenarios to protect their privacy. Fellow members of *The Book Club* have been combined and recast as composite characters to reflect the varied experiences of mothering addicted children. Still, the events in this book are true.

This is the counterintuitive story of how I found grace on the flip-side. It is a story about addiction, yes, and the familial challenges it describes are universal. Most importantly, it's a story about being a parent—and loving, caring, and providing for your children—in an uncertain world.

CHAPTER ONE
The Visit

The first time I saw my son in jail, he was only an hour's drive from home. We sat on opposite sides of a plexiglass window—Sam cuffed—a vacant looking, thickset officer towering over his shoulder. My throat had seized. I thought I might throw up. Or pass out. It was the handcuffs. My mind pictured those same hands learning to tie shoes, needing a Band-aid, wearing red mittens. Not needing restraint. I remember gripping the arms of the chair to steady myself, the flash of sweat above my lip, a stabbing pain in my heart.

The wall-mounted phone had been grimy with the sorrow of every mouth, ear and hand that had cradled it before me. It was my only connection to the boy who once planted milky lips over my ear to share secrets. As his mother, that jail visit was an experience I hoped to never repeat.

Today, I'd traveled 1600 miles to Adams County, Colorado, to pick up another phone. I'd see Sam's digital image for 30 minutes. He was worth every mile and every minute.

———

The road to Brighton is punctuated with hairpin turns. Through each steep switchback, Susan downshifts, her face furrowing in concentration as the engine growls into low gear. I ride shotgun, thanking my lucky stars for the dozen years my friend has lived in the Rockies. She can navigate these mountain roads without batting an eyelash.

"Is it possible to feel compassion and outrage at the same time?" I ask her, as the road flattens ahead. "Or love and disgust?"

A child psychiatrist, Susan holds advanced degrees in whining and tantrums. Convenient, I think, because right about now I feel like throwing one myself. "There's a highly clinical term for that, Lynda Lou," my old friend gives me a wink and conjures my college nickname. "It's called mixed emotions."

A month ago, I'd answered my phone and recognized an automated click-and-pause. The Adams County Correctional Facility in Brighton, Colorado was informing me that my son Sam was on the guest list. My heart sank.

"I don't know what to do first," I fume as I pull the printed directions out of my bag. "Hug him? Or smack him upside the head?" Neither of these are options, Susan gently reminds me. But that doesn't quash the urge.

By the time he was 21, Sam had already spent a night or two locked up somewhere, so I knew the drill. After the call, I sat at my kitchen counter, downloaded the visitor request form, uploaded a photo, and typed in my social security number. The Department of Corrections would run a background check before clearing me for a visit.

Inmates are limited to three visitors a month, scheduled during thin slivers of time on pre-ordained days. Five days after my application, another robo-call spat out the date and time of my assigned visit. *Take it or leave it*, the message taunted. In the meantime, Sam could be transferred to another facility on a whim. A trip to the Adams County Jail would be an act of blind faith.

I'd bought a plane ticket and called Susan, the only person in the State of Colorado I knew would understand. "Oh sweetie!" she cried out when I told her the news. "What can I do?"

"Say a prayer is all," I told her. "We won't have time to visit, but could I call you after I see him? I might need to hear your voice. It helps just knowing I'll be in your world."

I'd booked a room at an airport hotel, but Susan wouldn't hear of it. She met me in the arrivals lane at the Denver airport, adamant. "You're on my turf," she said as she tossed my overnight bag into the back of her Tahoe and slammed the hatch. "End of discussion."

Susan and her husband Burke shuttled between offices in Denver and a weekend house in Winter Park. I envied her rosy cheeks, western chill and effortless Patagonia chic. The wool overcoat I'd grabbed as I left Richmond felt East Coast uptight. Then, I pictured Sam in his baggy orange jumpsuit. What was wrong with me?

Evening fell in Colorado, but my watch and body read 9:30 p.m. I was wiped out.

Sam's story wasn't adding up; I briefed Susan on the drive. He'd call every week or two, always off to another concert, driving across two states to get there. How was he paying for tickets and gas? He never mentioned a job. I suspected he'd become an entrepreneur, a purveyor of controlled substances, and I told him so. He denied it but even from six states away it was clear to me he'd gotten tangled in a web of strong, sticky draglines.

Checking the directions, I spotted a low brick building from the highway. "That's it." I pointed to the exit sign ahead. "Take this one, here."

A mixture of bile and dread burned my throat as we passed a razor wire fence and entered the glass doors. I fell in line while Susan headed to the waiting room and found seats for us.

At the check-in desk, the officer scowled at my Virginia driver's license. I held my breath as she dragged her finger down the visitor list, stopped and tapped twice. "Monitor three. Eight-thirty-seven," she mumbled, motioning across the hall. "Wait there until you're called."

The worst thing I'd ever done in my life was drive my mother's station wagon around the block when I was 14. I volunteered at church, sent thank-you notes, and dropped the F-bomb only when pushed over the edge. Which brings us back to this day.

At home in Virginia that morning, a truck carrying a dozen Korean boxwoods with burlap-wrapped root balls had arrived right on schedule. My husband Robert and I had spent three years designing and building our shingle and stone house, and I was excited to oversee the finishing touches. Situated in a clearing behind a historic brick barn and paddock, the house was 12 miles from Richmond proper and a galaxy or two from Adams County. For me, the project had been an escape, a welcome distraction from Sam's drug use and legal problems.

I'd carved a niche business out of small garden design projects: kitchen gardens, poolside containers, window boxes and patio plantings. I was relieved that the only installation my Colorado trip would interrupt was my own. How could I have explained a jail visit to a client? I couldn't even explain it to myself.

My neighbor Annie, also a landscape designer, promised she'd meet the truck and crew for me. We'd been collaborating on our foundation plan for months, and I ran by her house the day I got the news from Adams. Even though I trusted her, I felt a little untethered telling Annie that Sam was back in jail. She listened without probing or judging and my racing heart calmed. "I'll do whatever you need, Lynda," she offered, and I knew she meant it.

I'd known Annie for 15 years, and her friendship had been a warm blanket around my shoulders more times than I could count. She'd gone through her own rough times too, and our backdoors were always open. When we moved to Roslyn Road, I was thrilled to learn that three-year-old twin girls lived behind us, the same age as my younger child, Charlotte. And through their friendship, mine with Annie blossomed.

It's beautiful. Annie's text had popped up when the plane landed. *The guys just left. Can't wait for you to see our sketches come to life.*

———

My mind returned to the waiting room, which charmed like a bus depot. An outdated television tilted off the wall, flickering above the mustard-colored chairs and speckled linoleum. A clutch of children, none older than nine, burbled and squirmed, playing musical chairs. Their mothers sat grim-faced and vacant. Stale cigarette smoke clung to a defeated man in a camouflage jacket slumped near the exit sign and mingled with resignation that hung in the air. Outside, a girlfriend paced back and forth, chewing gum, talking on her cell, and stabbing an arched red fingernail into the cold night air.

I took the chair next to Susan, who cupped her hand and whispered into my ear, "Why do you think the chairs are bolted down? So you can't hurl them? Like a weapon?" I smiled, thankful for a friend willing to cut the tension.

I shuffled through my mental Rolodex of gnawing worries, wishing I could bolt those down, too. During the flight from Richmond, I'd imagined every possible disaster.

What if I had the time wrong?

Or we couldn't find the jail?

What if my name wasn't on the list?

Or visiting hours had changed?

Because he faced charges in three counties, I half-expected the check-in officer to tell me he'd been transferred to another jurisdiction, making my trip—and Susan's—a colossal waste of time.

"I told Sam he needed to straighten up and fly right or this thing would play itself out in one of three ways," I counted on my fingers for emphasis.

"One: He'd wind up joining the Overdose Club."

"Two: He'd land in jail. Hellooo?"

"Or three: He'd find himself on the wrong end of a drug deal, and the police would find his body in a dumpster." I didn't add, chopped into small pieces and stuffed in a green garbage bag. It sickened me to let these thoughts intrude. "He didn't listen. Shocking, right?"

Susan shook her head gently, bearing witness. It felt good to be heard.

———

Nobody dreams of becoming a drug dealer. Sam was in the eighth grade when he encountered his first six-pack. But unlike most teenagers, alcohol hadn't held his attention. He eventually moved from pot to Percocet to heroin, which did.

By the time he was a high school senior, I would learn later that, Sam, my handsome, charismatic, born-salesman, was operating a fairly successful small business. Most dealers dabble at first, selling just enough to fuel their own habit. Small potatoes, they figure. What's the harm? Soon enough, though, the contact list expands, the client circle widens, the deals get bigger and the profit margin increases. With business booming, a steady job at ten dollars an hour holds little appeal.

I leaned into Susan, talking low, under the noise of the waiting room, picking up the thread of the story. "Sam explained it in a letter. He was walking to the store one afternoon when two drug enforcement agents pulled over, called him by name, and invited him to ride down to the station." It hadn't taken a crystal ball to see it coming. Finger pointing is an occupational hazard in this line of work, and Sam had used up his get outta jail free cards. "Now he's looking at four months or four years. We have no idea. But they're holding him here until sentencing. His dad's paid lawyers and posted bail too many times. Now, even he's drawn the line. Sam's got a public defender."

A crying baby, soothed by a mom no older than 18, prompted me to check the clock on the wall. 8:34 p.m.

Three minutes.

"Wish me luck." Susan patted my arm as I stood and stretched. "It's showtime."

I scanned the row of blank screens for monitor three and took my seat in the molded plastic chair, waiting for the blue light. At 8:37 p.m., Sam's face would appear and we'd have precisely 30 minutes to talk.

Two minutes.

Countdown.

Then the screen brightened. Sam was smiling. As I looked into those brown eyes, lit up just for me, my anger melted.

"Hi, sweet boy."

All I saw was the child I once knew, dressed in faded cargo pants, pockets stuffed with sand, rocks and crumpled bubble gum comics.

"Hi, Mama."

CHAPTER TWO

A Woolly Little Booger

When I was a baby, my mother would spread a patchwork quilt in our back yard and plop me down while she hung white sheets on the clothesline to dry. I didn't like touching the grass, she recalled, so I crawled around that square space, contentedly by her feet. I was a rule-follower, right from the start.

Before Sam was a year old, four of us formed what I fondly and firmly believe was *The Best Playgroup Ever*. I couldn't take in my good fortune; three great friends, Nell, Cameron and Lanier, and their beautiful babies, all ready to socialize.

When I hosted our first gathering, I carefully set out animal crackers and apple juice. Then, taking a page from my mother's book, I defined the play area with an extra large cotton blanket. Sam had other ideas when I plopped him down to stage a practice run. Its satin edge was enticing, a boundary ripe for the pushing. And he promptly crawled off to explore the world beyond.

———

Nobody dreams of *raising* a drug addict.

I've wanted to be a mother since I babysat for the Fowlers in middle school. The yearning grew and I prayed that, someday, the universe would bless me with children of my own. I've heard clergy members talk about their calling. Motherhood was one of mine.

Sam's dad Stuart and I were busy establishing careers and planning to buy our first house. We hadn't talked much about babies. I was a newly-minted recruiting coordinator for a law firm.

When the touch of nausea I'd attributed to new-job jitters persisted, I retreated to the ladies room, two flights up from my office, with a drugstore pregnancy kit. The test confirmed what I was hoping—for the time being—to rule out.

For three months, my days revolved around morning sickness, elevator trips, breath-mint chasers, and stolen glances in the mirror to wipe the spittle from my chin. Even as I drove the fourth-floor porcelain bus, I was ecstatic. Suddenly, one afternoon during the third trimester, my blood pressure skyrocketed, and I was admitted to the hospital with toxemia.

I still remember how Stuart's happiness filled the room when Sam made his debut the following night at 6:25 p.m., after an exhausting 24 hours, but blessedly, only a week before my due-date. I remember how peacefully he dozed in the crook of my arm, the pure smell of his skin—God, how I wish I could have bottled that scent. In that moment, I'd given my husband what he wanted more than anything in the world—a future quarterback or lacrosse player.

For both of us, it was love at first sight.

Sam's back and forehead were covered with the dark, downy hair peculiar to some newborns. The medical term is *lanugo*. Despite his furry first impression, there was no doubt in the hormone-ravaged, sleep-deprived myopia of this new mother—and I was sure that everyone in the hospital noticed the same thing—that this had to be the most insanely beautiful baby boy in the history of the world.

"He's a woolly little booger," Stuart beamed.

Overwhelmed with gratitude, my tears gave way to ragged sobs, until I wept so hard I could barely breathe.

My milk supply was ample. Sam guzzled, gulped, and swallowed so fast that, as soon as he became satiated, he'd projectile vomit clear across the room. It had been months of throw-up for both of us, so with the patient advice of our nurse practitioner, Marjorie, I switched to those cylindrical bottles with the plastic liners. "You squeeze out all the excess air," she coached over the phone.

By now, he'd shed the peach fuzz and his skin was smooth as honey from head to toe. In fits and starts, Sam and I settled into a routine—of sorts. I didn't know it at the time, but Marjorie would be holding my hand for the next 18 years.

I've scanned the rearview mirror for clues from those early days. A sensitive baby, Sam absorbed sights and sounds more fully than anyone I know. I seeded his crib with extra pacifiers we called "popeyes." And on fitful nights, I'd scoop him out of the crib and tiptoe downstairs.

Bathed in the jeweled light of Big Bird and Oscar, Sam and I forged a bond on our family room sofa. He'd nestle in the curve of my belly. As I rubbed his tiny back, he'd follow the characters, eyes wide as saucers, fondling one pacifier in each hand, and sucking a third; the rhythmic squeak-squeak-squeak marking time with our breathing. For two blissful years, until his sleep grew more predictable, the wee hours belonged to the two of us. Mother and son. Nothing else mattered.

Even as a teenager, beauty was more exquisite for Sam. Chaos, more chaotic. Pain, he found excruciating. *Was that a symptom?* I also scanned our family tree, looking for genetic clues. They must be hidden in the branches somewhere.

We soothe our fussy babies but as they grow, they must learn to soothe themselves. The lucky ones find solace in music or running; they scribble bad poetry or confide in a friend.

But, the unlucky? The ones overwhelmed by the noisy chaos of the world? Who lack the internal mechanism to carve out their own place of peace? The siren song beckons. And they stumble into the chemical equivalent of a Jacuzzi.

And it feels so good.

For a while.

CHAPTER THREE
A F#$@ing Full-Time Job

"Guess I don't need to ask how you are."

Sam leveled his weary chocolate eyes at mine. "I'm sorry you had to come so far." I could tell he meant it. "But I'm, um, glad to see you."

He had no idea how sorry I was. As that early spring night chilled and the stars showed themselves in the Colorado sky, my own sadness was mixed with a small comfort. Jail had an upside. For the next several months—or years—at least I'd know where he was.

"Now that I've detoxed, I'm doing better. Thank God that's over."

How could he be so upbeat? I'd be curled up in a ball, rocking in a corner. He's taking all this in stride. What do you say to your child when he's sitting behind bars? So how's the food? Do you like your pod-mates? Can you shoot baskets in the rec yard?

Detox is brutal. You're violently ill, throwing up one minute, sweating and shaking the next. And in jail there's no privacy. You're sharing a small space and a metal toilet with another inmate who may be detoxing, too.

Given all that, Sam looked better than I'd expected. He gets that from his father. Stuart could push a lawnmower in black socks and Bermuda shorts, his t-shirt soaked with sweat, and still cause a frisson of excitement among women in the neighborhood.

"They're giving me something for the anxiety now. It doesn't work all that well, but it's better than nothing."

For someone who's future hung in the balance, Sam possessed a calm compliance. I wanted to shake him and scream: *Do you realize you're facing four years in a freaking jail cell?* My eyes searched his face. A part of me wanted to remind him of what my parents told me hundreds of times: You lie down with dogs, you get up with fleas. And a part of me wanted to wash my hands of the whole situation. But the pull is too strong. Whether it's DNA or maternal instinct or just crazy-blind love, he'll always be my baby boy.

Sam paused and pointed to a spot at the top of the screen. "Mom, you've gotta look at the red light." A video camera was housed in the monitor. The conversation was being recorded, so we stuck to the facts. And we kept it light.

"How's Lily?"

Sam loves dogs like I love plants.

"I miss her already. She's at Scott's. He's got her food, her crate, everything she needs. And she loves his dogs, too."

What I really wanted to ask was *What's next? How long will you be in this cement cage?* I wanted to make sense of this legal mess, but I stuck to dogs, food and new friends. Behind Sam, other inmates milled around the pod, carrying on like a bunch of guys at the gym.

Thirty minutes passed in a blink. I added up the hours, the packing, the background check, the landscape pinch-hit from Annie, the expensive plane ticket, and my college friend changing her workday—all for a half-hour virtual visit that could have been Skyped.

And I'd do it all again in a heartbeat.

I told Sam I loved him. I prayed this would be a turning point in his life, a time for raw honesty, self-reflection and intense therapy. Even in jail, these resources were available to him. And if he wanted to paint a new picture for his future, he needed to use them. I didn't have time for a full-blown lecture. A one-minute pep talk would have to do.

Our visit left me without answers. And I longed to touch the child for whom I constantly grieved. A hug would have given me comfort. Him too. I could see that.

Instead, the monitor went dark. His handsome face vanished. I had no idea when I'd see him again. Or where. His case was unclear. During the same precious years his childhood friends would spend earning their college degrees, he could be locked in a place like this. The only person who could make that time meaningful was Sam. Could he see that?

I compiled my thoughts in a letter as soon as I got home:

> *Use this time to educate yourself. Read as much as you can on different subjects and become an expert in one. You might discover interests and talents you never knew you had. The only way you can work towards rehabilitation and recovery is through full disclosure. Cards on the table. Face up. You can't do this by yourself. Intensive work with a psychologist within the system is crucial. Support and consistency are key here. This will take a lot of hard work on your part, Sam. And I'm always here for you.*

Susan and I made our way back to Denver and stopped for dumplings at her favorite Chinese restaurant. As our plates arrived from the kitchen, I tried to make sense of Sam's situation.

"Over the years, he's lost every privilege that meant something to him, so surely, if this was only about us saying 'no' or setting limits, he'd have gotten the message a long time ago," I said. "This is so much bigger than him. Or me. Or all of us."

The visit left Susan shaken, though she tried to hide it. "Think about his day," I spurted, wildly waving my chopsticks. "Breakfast at 4:30 a.m., lunch at 10:20? Two people living in a five-by-eight cell? And Velcro shoes?"

Susan grabbed my hand across the table and held it tight. The warmth in her gesture released the tears I'd been holding back. She picked up an egg roll and paused before she bit into it. "How do you handle this, Lynda Lou?

"I've seen him in jail once before, about six years ago. So I thought I was prepared for today. But I feel sick. For God's sake, Susan. This is the little boy I dressed in Florence Eisman button-on-shorts and Peter Pan collars. And I'll be tucked into your 600 thread-count guest bed tonight while he's sleeping on a metal rack. That's a tough box to break down."

We sat together in silence for a moment, chewing on that.

———

Locals insist the giant white canvas roof of Denver's terminal, punctuated by tent poles, looks like a snow-capped mountain range. But as Susan's car approached the airport, I couldn't help but think: Teepee Village.

Whose brilliant idea was it to pitch a dozen super-sized tents and call it an airport terminal? WTF? I wonder when Sam'll buy his next plane ticket home?

From the departure lane, Susan jumped out of the driver's seat, hurried around curbside and motioned for me to drop my bag.

"Stay weak," she said, gathering me into a bear hug.

"Weak?" I questioned, squinting back.

"I mean it, Lynda Lou. Weak is where we ask for help. Some people call it vulnerable. But weak is why you called me. Weak is what puts you in the path of forgiveness and grace. Strong is too hard. I heard it in church last Sunday and I thought of you. Stay weak, sweetie. You let me know when you get home, okay?"

She squeezed my shoulder and turned to swing the car door shut. I already knew I adored her; but just then, a halo glowed over her head and a Hallelujah Chorus of gratitude sang in pure harmony. What had I done to deserve a friend who would spend a judgment-free evening with me at the Adams County Jail?

———

I settled into seat 32A and watched through the porthole as an orderly row of luggage rode the conveyor belt into the belly of the plane. The woman next to me swiveled her head in my direction, hungry for conversation. "Charlotte? Atlanta?" she probed.

"No, Richmond," hoping to leave it at that.

"My cousin lives in Richmond," she said brightly, just getting warmed up. "So, what do you do there?"

"I live out in the country," I said vaguely, as I opened the book in my lap and unwound the cord wrapped around my headphones, sending the universal signal for *leave me alone.* "I like the peace and quiet."

I was having a bad day. Make that a bad couple of decades. For over 15 years, I'd been consumed by Sam's *crisis du jour*. But the Adams County Jail had brought me to my knees. This wasn't just another crisis. This was Sam's life. And my reality, like it or not.

"Isn't that the truth? she persisted, amicably. "I love the outdoors. We just spent the week in Vail; those mountai…"

I clamped the headphones over my ears. Her voice was muted but her mouth kept moving. Ordinarily, I could talk to the backside of a barn. But, just this once, I was fresh out of nice.

You want the truth? I seethed in silence. *Frankly, Mrs. 32B, you can't handle my truth.*

I'm the mother of an addict, and it's a fucking full-time job.

CHAPTER FOUR

Codename: Book Club

We convince ourselves that addicts live on another, seedier side of town. And most likely, under a bridge. But they're sitting at our kitchen counter asking for a sandwich. They're opening the refrigerator and drinking milk from the carton. They're rifling through the pantry drawers looking for a midnight snack while making furtive phone calls.

When your child's an addict, words like *incarcerated, UT* (shorthand, *urine test*) and the slippery-sounding *recidivism* take up residence in your vocabulary, muscling out *team captain, graduation* and *full-scholarship*. Your social network expands, too. Instead of *coaches and scout leaders*, your contact list includes *public defenders, caseworkers and parole officers*.

I'd become proficient at whitewashing Sam's life, providing just enough information to be *technically* truthful. "He's out in Colorado," I'd say breezily, then change the subject.

"Hanging in there," I'd add, when pressed, as if he were facing midterm exams instead of a court date for felony drug possession.

And when the question of Thanksgiving or Christmas arose, I'd chirp, "We're all looking forward to being together!"

If there was a way to answer honestly, from the heart, I hadn't found it. Instead, I fudged the facts, determined to hide my shame. And in doing so, I was turning my pain inward, blaming myself: *Surely, a better parent could have avoided this train wreck.*

I didn't know another soul who had been pulled through this keyhole, so I threw my energy into minimizing the evidence. I mounted a cover-up. I smiled. I socialized, never giving a hint that too much of anything was wrong. I just focused on saving face, hiding the truth, blending in. *Nothing to see here, people. Move along.* But I was dying inside.

If I'd gone the other route and decided to match them, achievement for achievement, the conversation might have sounded like parody but would have been oh so true.

If they said: "We had all the children home for Nana and Poppy's anniversary."

I'd hit back with, *"Sam and I ate at Denny's before curfew at the halfway house."*

"He's applying to business school this fall."

"He's eligible for work release in three months."

"He passed the bar exam."

"He's aced every drug screen for 17 weeks."

"He's engaged to a darling girl from Raleigh."

"He made a friend at Narcotics Anonymous. And got his driver's license back."

So there!

The mothers and fathers of promising young adults had done nothing wrong, of course. Their children were simply on track, building their own lives. And mine wasn't.

The more I pretended, the more isolated I became. I guarded the full extent of my secret for years. *Who could I share everything with, after all?* So I carried my burden, for the most part, alone.

Sometimes, when the secret felt heavy and my smile wore thin, I wanted to rake my fingernails over their smug faces and mess up their hair for good measure. Because something was terribly wrong with my son. And—don't you get it?—that means something must be terribly wrong with me. With few to share my pain, it intensified until, rippling under my good-natured exterior was a toxic Three-Mile-Island rage.

————

One by one, they came out. Women whose lives I thought were ordered and nearly perfect, began to show themselves to me. Lang threw artful parties, Ruthie managed her family's foundation, and Sally masterminded charity auctions. Celeste nurtured a cottage business and her declining parents. All of them were raising children who basked in their reflected light. Radiant, contented wonder-women. Or so I'd thought.

Somehow we recognized each other. We shared a disquieting connection. We belonged to a club no one voluntarily joins. But the benefit of membership would be this: the pain we'd been bearing alone could now be shared.

I reconnected with these women in the oddest places, in unexpected moments. When Ruthie's call jangled my cell phone, I was pulling out of the drive-through lane at the bank. Our friendship began when we were young marrieds, but we hadn't crossed paths in ages.

"Well, as I live and breathe," I nearly shrieked, delighted to hear her voice, "to what do I owe this pleasure?"

We untangled the last few years before her voice grew solemn.

"Lynda, I know you've had some challenges with Sam and..." she hesitated. "We've been dealing with similar stuff. With Liz."

"Fill me in," I pressed, scanning the road for a good spot to pull over. I wanted to give her my full attention, but my head was spinning. What could she possibly need? A good math tutor? A career counselor? *A counselor* counselor? Surely, it wasn't serious.

When I last saw Liz, she was in middle school and had one of the lead roles in a community musical. During those years, Sam was at a therapeutic boarding school in the mountains of West Virginia. Thinking back, I'd felt more than a twinge of envy over Liz's accomplishments.

The worst crisis a family like Ruthie's would ever face was a kid hesitating on the brink of the real world, waffling between taking a job on Wall Street and applying to graduate school. *What was it?* I'd never heard a whisper of trouble. As far as I could tell, this family lived on a planet I no longer recognized.

"She said she needed help, told us herself, after her second DUI..." Her voice intermittent, I was having trouble comprehending what she was trying to tell me.

Liz?

DUI?

Help?

Her story couldn't possibly bear any resemblance to mine. *Could it?* I was sure nobody else had squirreled away shame like I had. But it did, and she had.

Maybe, just maybe, I wasn't alone?

That same thought had flickered through my mind several months back, but I'd dismissed it. Five of us had piled into a car bound for Charleston. We'd insisted it was time for a girls' weekend to visit a college friend. As we prattled over one another, our conversation landed on the child of a mutual friend. Someone alluded to underlying chaos, speculated on drug use. Sally, who'd been talkative early on in our seven-hour drive, went silent.

By the time we'd shifted to another subject, her silence sent a message. I'd done the same thing myself, countless times. *Could she be like me?*

Other times, the hint was a patently scripted report about a child in college. "And how's Mary doing?" someone would ask. Something in the mother's stumble, followed by "Oh! She's just fiiiiinnnnne," was a little too perky, a little too vague.

When I ran into Celeste, I immediately felt her unspoken understanding. I knew she'd struggled with her own demons, and the parking lot cocktail party that raged outside UVA's Scott Stadium seemed to be plucking her last nerve. Something in her eyes told me she wanted to connect on a deeper level. She'd heard, through Stuart, that we'd been struggling with Sam. But she didn't know how receptive I'd be to an opening. She didn't know how hard I'd been working on myself, digging deep inside my soul for stillness and peace. Later she told me she'd sensed I might need a chat about our children. But she didn't dare mention it in a stadium of 80 thousand people. Not then. It wasn't the right time.

Lang emerged when I bumped into her with her husband, Wallace, at a neighborhood restaurant. "My mother always said we should meet," she chattered. Lang grew up in Richmond. Stuart's mother and hers were old boarding school friends. "We have a lot in common," she said knowingly.

What did she mean? We both like yoga? We're both fascinated by acupuncture and energy healing? I would learn soon enough that, although we did share these restorative practices, both of our lives were unraveling.

Each of these conversational bridges inched us closer to the deepest connection of all, the one we'd left unspoken: some of our children were wrestling with substance abuse.

And so I'd found Lang, Ruthie, Sally, and Celeste. And as each one fell into my life, I realized that I'd been holding myself apart. I'd closeted this part of my story, certain it was more than anyone else could stomach.

It was Sally who finally connected the dots. Our phones started to ring. *Did you hear?* Celeste questioned Ruthie about Sally. *Did you know?* I quizzed Lang, when she mentioned Ruthie and Celeste. Sally gathered our emails and invited us to her house, tossing out suggested dates. We were eager to meet.

I felt like a survivor stranded on a desert island who discovers there are others. Are they friend or foe?

The five of us made it official. We would get together and attempt to schlog through our secret sludge. Our phone conversations revealed similar questions and fears. Were there guidelines out there for how to parent this madness?

We all feared late night phone calls and the terrible news they might bring. We slept braced for it. We still do.

We'd all been to Al-Anon, AA, or Families Anonymous, so we agreed to work the Twelve Steps. We formed our own support group, without folding chairs and fluorescent lights, and hoped to do the same good work that's done in church basements all over the country. Most importantly, we shared a goal: to reframe our relationship with our struggling children. Even if your life is blessedly free of addiction, the Twelve Steps are great, all purpose tools for dealing with any old messy relationship.

Each phone call established greater trust. And there were many. When we finally met, we stepped inside Sally's cheery family room; a fire warmed the space and a mouthwatering aroma simmered in the air. She'd set out a wooden platter of crackers and a block of cream cheese topped with pesto and roasted red peppers. As our hostess took drink orders, we settled around the coffee table. Ruthie and Celeste chose comfortable club chairs. Lang and I took the sofa.

Celeste threw up her arms, wildly waving us to order. "If y'all don't mind, I've done this a time or two." She'd been going to AA for years and knew the Twelve Steps backwards, forwards and in her sleep. Armed with sharpened pencils, highlighters, fresh Moleskine notebooks, like the first day of school, we were ready to tackle *The Book*. Celeste had instructed us to buy a copy of Melody Beattie's *Codependent's Guide to the Twelve Steps*. "A lot of what we call mothering is good old basic enabling," she explained. "You'll see."

"First off: The ground rules: What happens in Vegas, stays in Vegas," she said. "Complete confidentiality."

"What do I say if someone questions where I went last night?" Ruthie squeaked. "I can't even lie about what I had for lunch."

"Book Club." said Lang, definitively.

———

Book Clubs were popping up like mushrooms, so no one would question ours. "Hmmm," Ruthie pondered. "So what are we reading? What if they ask about that?"

"*The Help*," Sally tossed back without missing a beat. "If anyone asks, we're reading *The Help*, 'cause Lord knows, we all need it."

There's safety in numbers. I was convinced of that as I looked around the room. "First off, let's give the Cliff's Notes." Sally interjected, waving a ladle for emphasis. "I've got a pot of black bean soup on the stove. Ya'll can help yourselves in a minute. Let's go clockwise, but let me start. I need to throw the salad together."

She pulled up a footstool, sat down and looked at the floor, gathering her thoughts. "My son, George, came to us in the middle of the night. His father and I were dead asleep. It was July, right before his junior year in high school. He's our snapped-together child, a strong student, athlete, has a million friends.

"So we weren't prepared for what came out of his mouth: 'I'm snorting cocaine everyday, and... I think I might need help.' He'd gone from casual experimentation to a cocaine addiction in six weeks. His girlfriend had given him an ultimatum: 'Tell your parents or I'll tell them myself.' He struggled to cough up the truth, but in the end, that was the upshot."

"I'm telling you right now, a storm cloud rolled into that room. We were blindsided. Five days later, husband George loaded him into the car and drove ten hours to Florida.

I was proud he'd asked for help. He wouldn't have done it without his girlfriend's threat, God bless her. That was two years ago, and we're still pretty shaky."

The room was silent. Sally looked down and laughed nervously, almost startled to find the oven mitt in her lap. She picked it up, spoke into the thumb like it was a microphone. "Now, over to you Lang." She passed the mitt to her right and scurried in to the kitchen, still in earshot.

Lang picked it up, tapped it, awkwardly performing a soundcheck:

"testing,....one...two... three." She drew a big breath and launched right in. "I have a daughter, Ella. She's seventeen now, a junior. Clearly struggled with alcohol, got a DUI. Then the boyfriend came along and, thanks to his stellar influence, the alcohol morphed into pot, which climbed the food chain to heroin. Right now, she's willing to go for help, but her father's not too thrilled about spending a fortune on a place that's a plane ticket away."

Lang had a long career in pharmaceutical sales. She's athletic and outdoorsy. Happily remarried, she and her second husband retreat to the river on weekends with their dogs. Their families had blended, but not without some financial juggling. She looked down at her hands. "We're just not sure yet. He's a little worried about the money, especially when we looked at the statistics." She quickly passed the mitt to me like it was a hot potato.

"No place can guarantee recovery," Celeste interjected. "She might need a few rounds. He's got a valid concern."

Sally stepped back in the room and motioned to the group. "Dinner's ready. We'll move in here to eat. Lynda, you go next while everyone helps themselves to soup."

How do I make this under five minutes, I mumbled to myself. "Okay. We've been dealing with learning disabilities and ADHD since Kindergarten. And nobody tells you this, but ADHD and substance abuse can be connected. I couldn't have handled that news back then—I was just trying to survive the lower school stuff. But I'd read online about ADHD and thought, wow, these mothers are dealing with varsity level hyperactivity and inattention. Their children have a *diagnosed disorder,* right? And within months, guess what? Sam was diagnosed with the same thing. So now I'm one of those mothers. Our struggle finally had a name and my child's face was on it."

"Intense push-backs turned into a diagnosis of Oppositional Defiant Disorder. And by sixth grade, Sam was in a special boarding school, and Stuart and I had separated. The pot smoking started in eighth grade and, by ninth, he'd been through four schools."

I took a deep breath. Waiting for the judgement that never came. I'd said it and nobody had flinched. Instead they filled soup bowls, passed bread and salad. Quietly.

Listening. The exposure was exhilarating. I'd aired my dirty laundry and somehow I felt cleansed. I'd never laid out the facts, never spoken quite this openly to friends. Looking around Sally's kitchen, I realized I was surrounded, for the first time ever, by people who understood—because they were living it, too.

Sam had turned twenty-three that past winter. I'd felt alone since he started pushing back in third grade. Thirteen years and counting.

"….he's..a..a..heroin addict; he's been in and out of county jails. I live day to day waiting for the other shoe to drop." My hands were shaking from sheer, ragged emotion. I'd never had an altogether safe place to share. "Our parenting has been like parallel play; there's no collaboration, no consistency, and you can see where that's gotten us."

My throat seized as I tried to make a joke.

"So we have this child flopping around like a fish on a dock, and we can't communicate about it. If I was handling this alone, maybe I could find an answer. But we can't agree on the color of the sky. And it's killing me. I'm willing to put my own baggage aside and work together to find a solution. While he's throwing—whatever's within reach—on his wall to see what sticks. Stir in some financial tension," I said, nodding at Lang, "and you've got our recipe for disaster."

———

We took our places around Sally's kitchen table. We were the invisible casualties of addiction, a rare underground sisterhood, five women drawn into a circle of light. Celeste's daughter had been kicked out of school for pot. Ruthie's son had almost died of alcohol poisoning. Each of us mourned the child who might have been, the child who was desperately lost. We could not have known, not then, where these children were headed. In the upcoming decade we'd find ourselves attending the funerals of six young people within our children's worlds—two car accidents, three overdoses, one suicide.

The stats wouldn't tally for years. But that night, among the five of us, were eleven children, five of whom were addicts. They'd experimented with alcohol, Xanax, Ecstacy, pot and heroin. They'd struggled through eating disorders, been diagnosed with bipolar disorder and endured sexual abuse.

Collectively, we'd seen thirty-two counselors, attended AA, Narcotics Anonymous, Al-Anon, Families Anonymous, consulted with educational specialists, interventionists, psychologists, psychiatrists, tutors, an acupuncturist—even an energy healer. Our children had matriculated through wilderness programs, courtrooms, prison pods and halfway houses. They'd earned four DUIs, two and a half years of jail time, three years probation, five felonies, three high school expulsions, and three near-overdoses.

Together we'd spent over $350,000 on addiction. And not one of us was out of the woods yet.

———

"What can I get for you, Lynda?" Sally called over her shoulder as she reached into a cabinet for a glass.

Here was the tribe I'd never dreamed existed, their understanding a salve. I sank into their acceptance like a warm bubble bath.

"Not a thing, Sally." I answered. "Not a single thing."

"Open your books, now," Celeste guided. "Let's read the first step out loud."

We are powerless in the face of addiction.

It might seem like a simple concept, but we stayed on this chapter for months.

The mothering instinct is to fix, smooth over, repair, cover up, bandage, or, if all else fails, beat the crap out of anything that hurts our children. We think we can control what they eat, what they wear, their school, their friends. Then addiction lumbers in, sniffs the air for signs of weakness, licks its chops, sharpens its claws, and terrorizes us before knocking us flat and ripping our hearts out.

CHAPTER FIVE

Puzzle Without a Picture on the Box

I raised Sam and his younger sister Charlotte with generous doses of
laughter, love and organic fruit, on a gracious, tree-lined street where
neighborhood kids crisscrossed manicured lawns, threading in and out
of each other's houses. On any given Saturday, they'd gather on the swing
set in our backyard or ride Sting Ray bikes over our chalk-patterned
driveway, bright streamers trailing from their handlebars.

The wrought iron planters that flanked our front door overflowed
with impatiens in the spring and pansies in the fall. Inside, I'd done my
best to create a well-tended nest. Our children went to the private schools
nearby: what I'll call St. Boy's for Sam and St. Girl's for Charlotte. On
weekends, Stuart and I shuttled them to sports practices and dance lessons or drove the hour to Charlottesville to see a University of Virginia
football game. These were happier times.

We weren't breaking new ground during those Roslyn Road years.
Families from Darien to Durango have lived this life for generations. Still,
ours matched the picture I'd carried from my own childhood, right down
to the starched linen napkins I used for dinner parties. It was a pret-

ty, stable life; my love for my family trimmed out in Benjamin Moore's *Silver Cloud.*

One day, that rosy picture would be my undoing. But at the time, I felt intensely grateful. My children were healthy. I had a handsome, hard-working husband, a comfortable house, and a close circle of friends. Boo-boos, Band-Aids and bullies were child's play compared to the turmoil that lay ahead.

———

When your child starts school, you have no idea who you're bundling off with a backpack and a lunchbox. A kindergarten teacher could paint a giant question mark on each precious student's head. Yours could be a National Merit scholar or a middling student with a killer curve ball. Every parent entertains hopes of untapped potential. But early on, some of us notice the wagon is wobbling. And pretty soon, the wheels start to fall off. One by one.

My first clues were subtle: a teacher ducking his head into the car window as I crept through the carpool lane. "Would you mind calling me tonight?"

I started getting notes home in Sam's backpack, math tests with red ball-point x-marks skipping down the page and report cards with entire columns of NS, Not Satisfactory. "Pink" slips followed in late fall, as the three-wheeled wagon zig-zagged, ever so slightly off course.

"We'd like to suggest a little tutoring."

"We have a special group meeting on Thursdays."

"We'd like you and your husband to come in for a talk."

By spring, we'd decided that Sam should repeat kindergarten at St.

Boy's. We hoped he'd outgrow the impulsivity and learn to pay attention. Mrs. Wilson, his God-sent kindergarten teacher, agreed to deliver the news. She took him to lunch for pizza and a milkshake.

"Sam, honey?" she began. "Big trees need deep, strong roots to help them grow. You'll grow up to be a big tree someday, Sam. And I believe the best way to make sure your roots grow Superman strong is for you to go through kindergarten again next year."

Sam listened respectfully, then went about his business as if he was heading right on to first grade like everybody else. At the time, we assumed his kindergarten do-over was the biggest hurdle he'd face in school.

If only.

Kindergarten: The Sequel, was an uphill climb. Mrs. Smith managed Sam's do-over with kid gloves. Still, each day brought new challenges. And there was no quick fix. I plucked every morsel of information from the more-experienced-parent grapevine and quickly discovered a pattern. You start in the extra-help group and advance to after-school tutoring, while parents set up additional teacher conferences. When that doesn't work, you look beyond the school walls for a solution. And the quest begins.

The first stop is an audiologist to check hearing and auditory processing. Does your child hear like Charlie Brown heard his teacher? *Wah, wah, WAH, wah.* Next, the neurological consultant administers tests and converts your child's brain into a series of pie charts and graphs. You hold your breath while the good doctor interprets the findings, praying the terms "brain damaged" or "beyond repair" don't come up in the summary.

You scan the horizon for the psychologist, psychiatrist, book, diet, behavior expert or educational consultant who may hold the answer. Yet you feel guilty for treating your child like a problem in need of a solution. If you stop looking, you're irresponsible, or at best, unconcerned. If you keep looking, are you focusing on the problem or the child?

Are you overreacting?

Underreacting?

You're damned if you do and damned if you don't.

Is it something that might run its course, like the flu?

Won't he just grow out of it?

Next comes medication. Short-acting, long-acting, extended-release, small dose, large dose, tri-cyclics, mono-cyclics. It's a crap shoot.

"Let me know how he does with this," the doctor says, scribbling a prescription. How can I know?

In the 1990s, before meds had to be school-nurse registered and administered, I'd drop Sam's pill into a ziplock baggie, slip it in his lunchbox, and hope for the best. The medication had a short half-life so, by afternoon dismissal, it had worn off. As the medication left Sam's system, the impulsivity and inattentiveness intensified. He became more hyperactive, like the volume had been turned up. Doctors call this "rebound." Rebound turned afternoon play dates into a minefield.

How could I send a buzzing, volatile child off with a friend after school? How could I know he wouldn't pick up a golf club and swing it within a quarter-inch of the other child's eyelashes? I wouldn't. If he were to go anywhere, with anyone, he needed another dose. Do I drop another pill into another ziplock baggie and deliver it to the mother of the child who invited him? Was it her job? Would she think I'm neurotic?

If they're going to the playground or the petting zoo, do I chase them down, pretend he forgot his jacket, pull out a bottle of water and a pill from my coat pocket? And in one neat sleight of hand, make him swallow the pill, nobody the wiser?

A mother facing this predicament starts thinking like a special forces operative, highly trained in covert missions, parading undercover as a sweet, thoughtful Super Mom, if only a tad overly attentive. It was a double life; and it was exhausting.

When strategic maneuvers became too much, I tried a basic, more direct approach. I'd tuck notes in his lunchbox, reminding Sam to take his medicine. Still, most days, the pill boomeranged back home. Around four o'clock in the afternoon, I'd play the messages on the answering machine. And just as I opened the lunchbox to find the wrinkled baggie with the little pill still inside, I'd hear the teacher's voice asking me to give her a call.

Message.

Pill.

Cause and effect.

On medication, Sam was like most any other little boy—rambunctious but not too reckless. The reckless boy, the Sam without medication, was a collection of symptoms. His driven, impulsive behavior was the manifestation of his yet-to-be-diagnosed disorder. The boy on medication was the true Sam. The Sam that Sam wanted to be. The Sam free of symptoms. On medication, Sam was like a child with asthma after he's used his inhaler, breathing freely, temporarily relieved of his disease.

Was this a genetic predisposition?

Mostly ADHD?

A result of toxemia at birth?

Crappy parenting?

As the questions swirled in my mind, I clung to one sentence on page seven, paragraph three of an earlier doctor's report: Stuart and

I "appeared to be loving parents with the child's best interest at heart."

———

Still, I faced my critics. I heard everything from, "You're just lazy," to "You're medicating him because you can't be bothered," to "He'll be a zombie. You'll take away his personality." And from at least one grandparent, "Tell him it's a vitamin."

It's never too early to start fudging the truth, right?

While medication was a gift, it didn't solve Sam's learning problems. During third and fourth grades, we constantly propped him up, nudging and gently pushing him forward. We employed after-hours tutors, trying to get as much work done at school, in an effort not to bring the conflict home. Fourth grade brought many strategy sessions about academics and behavior.

We already knew a hundred possible reasons for the unacceptable behavior. Which ones were valid though? And of those, which ones could we address?

Maybe the rigorous curriculum at St. Boy's was *too* rigorous?

Maybe his dad and I put too much pressure on him?

Maybe Sam put too much pressure on himself?

Maybe he'd carved out a bad name for himself at school and a fresh start was just the ticket?

Maybe he'd thrive with a Montessori approach?

Or maybe, he was just pushing our buttons and enjoyed being a pain in the ass?

I checked out dozens of resources from the library and came up with at least that many more possible explanations, from food-additives to allergies. The tower of books on my bedside table ranged from *The Feingold Cookbook For Hyperactive Children* to a slew of resource material from T. Berry Brazelton.

As one mother said to me about her own child, "Not only am I his mother, I have to be his psychologist, psychiatrist and pharmacist, too."

I was prepared to uproot him, leaving *our* friends to do what was best for him. If you'd asked me a year before, I might not have been ready to let go of the image I'd mapped out for his happy childhood: Colonial Day, the middle school science fair, the weekly chapel services, the blue blazers that upper schoolers wear on their field trips, the yearbook photos, the junior/senior dance, upper school mission trips and awards ceremonies. Whether I wanted to admit it or not, I'd scrolled through twelve years of cherished traditions when I dropped him off on the first day of kindergarten.

We all like to hang on to the familiar. That's why traditions endure. At this school, I could picture his future. But if he went somewhere else, that picture blurred. I couldn't see what might be around the corner with the same clarity that I already thought I knew at St. Boy's.

Some children and their parents cling to competitive learning environments. By the time they've paid for the tutoring sessions, the summer reviews, the testing and the educational consultants, they could have purchased a small, private island in the Caribbean. The child has become a strung-out mess, convinced beyond a shadow of a doubt they're sub-par. The other members of the family are not far behind.

I was working a puzzle without a picture on the box. I wanted to see a smiling boy in a navy blazer picking up an award or two at graduation. I would learn later that this is called "private-logic" or "Lynda-logic."

And the picture I wanted to see was *my* picture, not Sam's.

CHAPTER SIX

Losing My Religion

"The human mind is more likely to hold on to a painful memory than to cherish a good one..."

I was waiting for my hair color to process one morning at Salon Belmont when that sentence jumped off the page of an outdated issue of *Redbook*, a word arrow straight to my heart. As a mother, I would like to pick and choose the moments that stick with my children. But, I know better. I am powerless over their memories.

After fifteen years of emotional heavy lifting, my stomach still knots when I think about the afternoon on Roslyn Road, the day I seared a painful memory into my children's tender psyches. By my own calculation, I'd need a dozen hands of Go-Fish, five Easter egg hunts, a seven-layer birthday cake, a Labrador puppy—and perfect parenting every day thereafter—to undo the damage I'd done.

I prayed they would forget that horrific day. But *I* never will.

—

I grew up in South Carolina where, for good reason, any unholy display of anger is called *losing my religion*. My own mother never did. At least I never witnessed her completely losing it. Still, I reminded myself later, every mother yells. And the ones who look you in the eye and swear on a stack of Bibles they've never had their last nerve plucked? Never turned into Ursula the Sea Witch, unhinged? Can they possibly be telling the truth?

Years later, the memory still pierced me. I would never know what young mother had been pushing a stroller past our house that day, or which teenager was within earshot. I couldn't find a way to forgive myself, so one day, looking for peace, I brought it up over lunch with my friend Miriam, our across-the-street neighbor back then. Miriam knew we'd had more than our share of ups and downs on Roslyn. And she and I had remained close. "I'm almost scared to ask you," I began. "But I can't shake it. Do you remember that day when I lost it? Could you hear me when it happened? Or did we just talk about it later?"

"Open," she said without hesitation, flinging her hands up towards the heavens, as if she'd anticipated my question. "The windows were definitely open. I heard *everything*."

If I was looking for sugarcoating, Miriam wasn't offering.

—

Sam was ten. Charlotte was six. A wide-eyed kindergartner with an affable nature, my little girl wanted nothing more than to please me and everyone around her.

Each day brought new promise. That is, until the irritations of the morning piled higher than our dirty laundry. Most days before school, I traveled up and down the stairs too many times to count, prodding Sam, gritting my teeth.

"Time to get up, sweet boy."

"Did you pack your backpack?"

"Where are your shoes?"

"Eat some breakfast, pleeeease."

"Huuurry! You don't want to hold up the carpool!"

One minute, he was tying his shoes and the next, plundering the pantry for an after-breakfast snack.

Mornings with school-aged children are universally fraught with chaos. But when your child has an undiagnosed case of Oppositional Defiant Disorder (ODD) with a side order of hyperactivity, hold the attention span (ADHD), the chaos becomes turbo-charged.

I'm sure Stuart wasn't the only father who, at a loss to explain his child's behavior, chose instead to scrutinize the mother. *Why can't you handle this? What's wrong with you?* But the more I hurried Sam, the more he dug in his heels. And the harder he dug, the more Stuart second-guessed me. And the more Stuart second-guessed me, the more I doubted myself.

Why couldn't I handle this? How does everybody else get to school on time? We'd been a family once. But now we were a collection of chain reactions. We bickered. We simmered. We snapped.

And as the pressure mounted, I became desperate.

When I'd finally sweep the children out the kitchen door and into their carpools, I'd stand at the counter with a second cup of coffee, regrouping from the emotional and physical madness before loading the breakfast dishes and heading out for errands and a workout.

Back at home, my day almost always included the red message light on the phone, flashing wildly. I would replay them, one by one, each message more urgent than the next:

Sam forgot his book.

His jacket.

His permission slip.

and, Mrs. Harrison?

Could we discuss his quiz?

His "pink slips"?

His playground behavior?

Back in the car, I'd run up to school with the book or the jacket. I'd careen into the office with baked beans for the canned-goods drive. Then I'd circle back for a teacher conference. The words might vary from week to week, but the message would be the same. He's unfocused and disruptive. I felt like a one-woman pit crew who'd raced in to patch a punctured tire and get my driver back on track.

———

Ten years later, when I recounted this cyclical pattern in Book Club one night, Celeste brightened. "The pattern didn't change because you didn't change, right?" She studied Ruthie and Lang who, just then, were busy poking pita chips into Sally's black bean and cilantro hummus dip. "We've all done it. Our children's lack of attention becomes our problem."

"Yep," I said. "I used to turn myself inside out like a dirty sock to bail Sam out. Why did I get on that whirlygig, in the first place? Who put me on call 24/7, like a firefighter, ready to jump into my boots and slide down the pole, any hour, day or night?"

"I remember one particular third grade field trip. The Capitol. Every boy was required to wear his red St. Boy's sweater that day. And guess who forgot his? Did the school call Stuart about the damn sweater? Of course not."

"So what did you do?" Sally was genuinely hoping to borrow a page from my codependent scratch pad.

"Yeah," said Lang. "How'd you handle that one?"

"I rushed right over to the school, sweater in hand. In those days, I was jumping through hoops just to check the boxes—for whom exactly? The lower school receptionist?"

Lang cracked up. "The picture day mom?"

"No no no, it's the Snack Coordinator!" Ruthie added. "You don't want to piss her off."

"Seriously, I'd never stopped to consider the role I'd played in sabotaging myself. Then one day, after years of counseling, it dawned on me. What made me think I had to be Sam's rescuer, backup plan, and safety net?"

"We've all got to dial down this hovering nonsense," Celeste paused, then whispered to draw us in. "But we're terrified, aren't we?"

"Damn straight," I bristled. Sometimes, Celeste acted like the boss of us.

Sally came back for more, still confused. "Celeste, there's a big leap between getting a "pink slip" for forgetting your red sweater and getting convicted for dealing."

"Is there?" Celeste asked. "Doesn't it boil down to personal responsibility? If someone's cushioning the blow when you forget your red sweater in third grade, how does a kid learn logical consequences? God invented "pink slips" to keep them out of jail. For a child to want success, he's got to know failure."

If only I'd had Celeste on my team back then. I might have realized that nobody ever died from wearing a pilled red sweater, pulled from the lost and found. But when every day brought a new curve ball back then, I'd become shell-shocked. *Remind me again what I was doing before I was interrupted by your latest crisis, Sam?*

"What should you have done?" Sally persisted.

He forgot his red sweater? They've got a field trip to the Capitol? I should have said, "I'd love to help out, but I have an appointment. I'm sure there's a red sweater in the Lost and Found. Ask Sam to rummage through and find one. He can return it before dismissal."

"And you know what? That appointment? It could have been a long training run. Lunch with an old friend. An appointment with myself should be every bit as legitimate as an appointment with anybody. If I wouldn't cancel on the dentist at the last minute, why would I cancel on myself?"

"There are always a half-dozen red sweaters in the lost and found and if Sam has to wear one two sizes too small? Tough. Maybe he'll re-member it on the next field trip. I learned to notice what happens when I change my response. Remember Nadia, the surgeon? Her son was in Sam's class? What do you think she would have done if she was in the middle of resecting a perforated bowel?"

———

On that particular open-windows Tuesday, another call from school had set me on edge. The three of us had just trooped into the house from afternoon carpool. It had been my day to drive. We had a twenty-minute turnaround: Charlotte had a birthday party at four; Sam was due to meet his tutor at 4:30. I'd worked it all out in my head. I'd dole out a snack and they'd regroup while I wrapped the present.

I asked Sam to run upstairs to get his math notebook and told Charlotte to fish her favorite leggings from the laundry basket perched on the bottom step. Everybody had their marching orders. I'd set my plan in motion.

Only Sam wasn't buying it.

"Nope," he called over his shoulder, casually. "Not going."

"You are going," I countered.

Later, I would learn that ODD kids relish this kind of direct opposition. I'd issued an engraved invitation to a knock-down-drag-out power struggle.

My patience was frayed, but I'd missed the clues that I was heading toward a point of no return. The corrosive teacher comments, the birthday mom—who'd called twice to confirm that Charlotte was coming to the party—and the bill from the child behavior specialist which our insurance company had just rejected, all rattled around in my head while I tried to tie a perfect grosgrain bow.

Jesus?

God?

Does anybody in this house hear me?

Just that morning, Stuart had thrown up his hands as he left early for work. Again.

Am I the only ringleader trying to make sense of this circus?

A switch flipped, and I started to scream.

"Get upstairs *now!*"

Only this time I didn't stop. I screamed until it swallowed me up, repeating myself like a scratched record.

"NOW!"

"Now, Sam, Now! *GET UPSTAIRS NOW!*"

The room shrank from view, and I lost all awareness of my surroundings.

"GODDAMMIT SAM, NOW!"

My fury escalated until I was yelling loud enough to be heard clear up in D.C.

I was no longer an angry mother.

I *was* anger.

At some point, I remember looking over my shoulder and asking myself this:

Is it October?

Dear God, please let the windows be closed.

My throat was sore, my body limp.

That's when I noticed Charlotte, cowering in the hall, her bottom lip quivering and plump tears tumbling down her pink cheeks.

She was terrified.

Of *me*.

A pair of neatly folded lavender leggings lay on the floor beside her.

The wallpaper and furniture came back into focus only when I heard the phone ring. Unconscious, I picked up the receiver.

"Are you ... all right?" my friend Camille asked.

Where am I?

What just happened?

How does she know?

My shame blistered as I took in the hideous scene that had unfolded in our cheery orange-and-white kitchen. Guilt in the form of nausea grabbed me and wouldn't let go. I'd been unable to control my rage, and I was exposed.

Was I crazy?

Even Joan Crawford had good intentions in the beginning.

Was I some kind of nightmare mother? I hadn't laid a hand on either one of them, but my screams—I'm sure—had stung like a slap.

In hindsight, I wonder how I'd suppressed my rage as long as I did. I'd been plugging the dike with my finger, and the goddamn dam had finally burst.

We all get angry, but most days, we manage to keep the wheels on the road. On that October afternoon, I skidded across four lanes and left tire marks on the pavement before landing upside-down in a ditch.

And I hadn't seen it coming.

Sam missed his tutoring session, fifty dollars flushed down the toilet. He spent the remainder of the afternoon in his room with a chair up against the door. Charlotte was a no-show at the birthday party, after we'd accepted—*twice.*

———

That night, as Charlotte crawled under the covers, the psychological toll was evident in her eyes. Once again, she was an innocent bystander, an eyewitness to hysteria. And she'd just seen her mom lose her shit.

"My sweet girl," I whispered. "I'm so sad about what happened today. I know you were scared. It scared me, too. I promise to never, never, ever yell like that again."

She seemed to be thinking; her breathing—tiny whispers—the only sound between us. Finally, she answered weakly. But, oh, so strong.

"I think, um, you were the 'R' word today, Mommy."

"The what?"

What is she talking about?

"You know that word you're always saying?"

"Hmmm, the 'R' word?"

I tried to take on a playful tone. *Did she mean rage, rant, on-a-rampage? What?*

"Mommy, you were a wreck."

Out of the mouths of babes.

"Yes, I was." *And I still am.*

I kissed her four times on the forehead, gave her a bear hug, told her I loved her—to Mars and back—and switched off the light. She managed a sigh and rolled over, all cried out.

The three of us were shaken from the afternoon's events. Sam willingly brushed his teeth and climbed into bed with Bo, our golden retriever, at his feet. The lights were already out when I entered his room.

"Sam? Are you still awake?"

He was groggy, but I hugged his neck hard, burying my face in his pillow. Kissing his cheeks and forehead, my tears soaked the pillowcase.

"I lost it, Sam. And I'm sorry. It's not all your fault. I have a lot on my mind. I love you and Charlotte, and I'd never hurt either one of you. Please, let's start over. Forgive me? Everything will be all right, I promise."

"I forgive you, Mama. Love you. Night," he mumbled.

Staring at his silhouette in the darkness, I rubbed his back until I could hear the soft, steady breathing of my sleeping son. I tiptoed out of his room, knowing that we were far from all right.

That night, curled in a fetal position under the reassuring weight of my duvet, I couldn't sleep. I didn't recognize the woman who'd been yelling. She frightened me. I knew I needed help. And I knew one more thing, with certainty. The struggles we'd been having with Sam were not the garden-variety stuff of parenting a spirited boy. That open-window day forced me to question everything. Something was terribly wrong. But what, exactly, was it?

Long before their substance-abuse emerges, addicts are often a handful as children. I would learn this years later. These children require Ph.D. level parenting, with airtight consequences and consistency. You can't just wing it. But back then, nobody had the foresight—or maybe it was the heart—to tell me that my third-grader had all the hallmarks of an addict-in-the-making.

But I recognize the signs now.

Insatiable.

Impatient.

Impulsive.

Volatile.

And with a conscience made of Teflon, he was impervious to the gentle scoldings, time-outs, and loss of privileges that worked with most of the other children on my block. How do you think he got to Adams County?

When I revisit that Tuesday in October, I try to pinpoint what had ignited my rage. What pushed me over the edge? Whatever he'd done, Sam hadn't caused my explosion on that particular day. Each frustration that had been rattling around within me, within our house, our family, were little puzzle pieces swirling in a pretty box. And on that day, they spilled out, scattered on the table, then magically snapped into place.

The message read in bold letters:

This.

Is.

Madness.

My confidence as a mother was eroding. My marriage was creaking and moaning under the pressures. And my life was looking less and less like the rosy picture I carried around in my head.

And he hadn't even taken his first bong hit.

CHAPTER SEVEN

The Stone School

M*other dear, I'd like to leave all my friends and enroll in the school across town,* said no child ever. I've yet to meet a fourth-grader who'd choose to trade friends, teachers and familiar surroundings to be the new kid. Once you've found a match, you figure the school box is checked.

It's the parents' job to know when to hold 'em and when to fold 'em. And lacking a crystal ball, that decision is never easy. By Sam's fourth-grade year, I was ready to play a new hand. I had to face facts; St. Boy's was not right for him.

I had to break this news to a child whose stubborn opposition had earned him a diagnosis. It was my job to convince him to consider a school where he didn't know a soul. I'd need him to walk into that school, greet an adult stranger, make eye contact, offer a firm handshake, and sit down for a candid one-on-one interview. Finally, I had to inspire that child to persuade the unknown adult behind the big desk that he'd be an excellent addition to their already tight-knit educational community.

This is the same child who'd come undone when Sour Cream and Onion was the only bag of potato chips left in the assortment.

"It's like I'm trying to pass a bad check," I blurted to a friend, days before the interview. The check itself was adorable, but the account had insufficient funds. Sam's self-esteem had taken a hit in the competitive environment of St. Boy's. The school and the child had been an educational mis-match. And when children feel overwhelmed in a classroom, they can turn disruptive—anything to take the focus off the lessons they're *not* learning."

"After repeated failures, a child will stop trying altogether," one compassionate teacher explained. "They can laugh off a bad grade, if they didn't study. But if they pour heart and soul into that spelling test—and they still fail? Then their worst fears have been confirmed. *I really am dumb,* they think. School literally becomes painful; they'll do anything to avoid it."

———

The school search was on. The closest public school packed thirty fifth-graders into a classroom. While Sam was busy disrupting the crowded class, he'd slip through the cracks and fall further behind academically. The school that specialized in learning disabilities didn't start until sixth grade. Until then, a private school offered small class sizes and plenty of extra help. Just what Sam needed.

This left just three schools. The first two, I'll call Coke and Pepsi. We already attended Coke (aka St. Boy's), a private single-sex Episcopal school. Six miles west, the co-ed Pepsi was academically outstanding and non-denominational. If Sam couldn't handle Coke, he'd never survive at

Pepsi either.

My only hope was Dr. Pepper. Also co-ed, Dr. Pepper supported children with learning differences, offering small classes and a gentler academic pace. Dr. Pepper was already a strong school, but changes were brewing. An anonymous donor had stroked a substantial check. Now, flush with funds, the school had undertaken an ambitious expansion with new buildings and a stepped-up focus on "academic excellence."

If Sam wasn't a good fit, I figured the admissions department at Dr. Pepper would tell me. Perhaps they could even suggest better options.

I assumed all schools practiced open and honest communication with parents. With a shared goal of developing young minds, why wouldn't they? How naive I was. At private schools, employees are often bound by unwritten internal rules that restrict what they can tell a parent. And the most crucial message—the news that a child would be better served elsewhere—tops the sticky-subject list.

School advisors sometimes beat around the bush, they drop hints, but they rarely are allowed to cut to the chase. Meanwhile, you assume everybody's laid their cards on the table. Even when it's hard to swallow, the truth is always in your child's best interest. If you don't believe me, try asking your school resource counselor to recommend a more suitable school. When my friend Cece did, she was shocked by the answer: "We're not in the business of recruiting for other schools."

———

I set up an interview at Dr Pepper, and lobbed the concept to Sam the night before. He paused for a split second.

"I'm not going to *that* school."

I tried to act casual.

"Oh, I dunno, I hear the teachers bring their dogs to class sometimes," I said, checking his reaction. "They sit up front, at the teacher's feet," I embellished. "And every day, one student gets to take the dog outside."

Sam cut his eyes in my direction. "What's the dog's name?"

Now I had his attention, but I was just making shit up.

"Why don't we ride out there tomorrow and find out?" I ventured, holding my breath. "And guess what, Sam? You get to miss your last class. I'll pick you up at 1:30, and you'll be out of school for the rest of the day."

"K," he mumbled, barely looking up from his Nintendo joystick.

The next afternoon, as we pulled into the parking lot, Sam's eyes widened. The row of stone buildings looked nothing like his brick school. He slumped in the front seat. At that moment, the defiant boy who could drive me to distraction, looked small and scared.

"We've got a deal, remember? We're just going to chat a little and ask about those dogs, got it?"

"No test?"

"No test, sweet-boy. I promise."

When we walked into the Admission Director's office, Sam's resistance was palpable. The director greeted us with the artificial smile of a used-car-salesman, the kind that sets off alarm bells in any intelligent child. He took my paperwork, checked that Sam's application was in order, led Sam back into his office, then shut the door.

My breathing shallow and my hands sweating and shaky, I took a seat in the hallway and tried to focus on a current issue of their alumni magazine. Antsy, I popped up to peruse the bulletin boards that lined the walls. As I picked out familiar faces from church or the pool, I found myself saying a little prayer for a fresh start in beautiful surroundings. I imagined new friends, more nurturing teachers, Sam playing a sport, even. We'd been spinning tires for so long; it was time to get towed out of the ditch, hose off the mud and get back on the road. Dr. Pepper could be our answer.

I'd cautioned the admissions assistant that Sam wasn't enthusiastic about leaving his school. The transition might be bumpy, I hinted, then quickly added how I felt sure, however, he'd throw himself right into the mix. The assistant cheerfully waved me off. "Old-hat for us," she chirped. "We see it all the time."

So, from my perch on the hallway bench, I allowed myself to be seduced by the prospect of a new life in a new school. In truth, I had no control over Sam's interview, or whether Dr. Pepper would accept him. Still, happy images streamed through my mind, floating like downloaded photos into their tidy, new desktop folders.

It's called "creating the story." And we all do it.

We go on a first date and start to picture the wedding. Or a lottery ticket triggers an imaginary spending spree. Sometimes these stories are harmless daydreams. But when daydreams run wild, they sap our energy. We wind up living the story twice. Once in a fantasy world and, a second time, when the events unfold in real life. We spin a cotton candy story, ignoring the possibility of a black licorice ending.

There on the bench, I created the story, the easy adjustment, the positive report card, the dog in the classroom.

That's it!

I stood up, struck by a sudden insight!

We just need a stone school instead of a brick one!

"Mrs. Harrison?" the used-car-salesman peered around his office door, looking unharmed. Sam emerged, giving nothing away. "It was a pleasure to meet you both; we'll be in touch." His voice was bright and sing-songy.

I shook his hand and wondered if we'd been ever-so-politely dismissed. As we walked down the polished hallway to the door, a ticker tape clicked off in my head.

Didn't they need me to fax transcripts?

When would we have our next meeting?

Would Sam get a campus tour?

Or visit a classroom?

I had so many unanswered questions, I assured myself that the interview was a warm-up, a free consultation. I wasn't in a position to press the admissions department. Surely, I figured, he'd call tomorrow to set the formal application process in motion.

But tomorrow came and went.

The summer reading list from St. Boy's came home in Sam's backpack.

Final assembly instructions followed.

All around me, mothers buzzed with news of camps and family vacations.

Sam had all but forgotten his visit to the Stone School.

I held onto my secret alone and continued to "create the story" which, by now, was a puffy pink cloud of spun sugar onto which I'd pinned my sanity.

I checked phone messages daily. When the Stone School called, I wanted to respond promptly.

I looked at my calendar.

Four weeks.

I'll give them one more day.

Nothing.

Maybe they were busy, I reasoned.

I didn't want to appear anxious. So I resisted the urge to call.

Fifty-seven days after Sam's interview, I broke down and dialed the number. The decision-makers weren't available, the receptionist assured me, still chirping. "But someone will contact you real soon." They were in the process of sorting out their class roster for the upcoming year.

I'd put all my eggs in this one basket because it was the only basket I had. And it didn't feel right to keep school-shopping until we'd heard yea or nay from the Stone School, our first choice. This was Sam's best bet, the closest we could come to our next solution. Again, I prayed for a miracle.

Ten days later, it was June. I couldn't imagine what was taking so long. Maybe Sam landed on a waiting list. I called the school, once again, and asked for the admissions department.

I was surprised when the director answered the phone.

"Mr. Used-Car-Salesman?" I asked. "I was wondering if you have any news about Sam?"

There was a short silence on the other end.

"Sam Harrison? We met you about nine—no it was ten weeks ago?"

More silence.

Had my phone died?

"Oh," he said cooly, clearly caught off guard. "The class is full."

More awkward silence.

Did that mean he hadn't been accepted? Surely, I'd missed a step. Or was the class full for now, and he'd have a more accurate number in a few weeks?

He never spoke Sam's name. He never thanked us for our interest, wished us luck, told us to go fly a kite, or pound salt. He never suggested an alternate route. He acted like we'd never met. Clearly he'd been hoping we'd just go away.

I was too stunned to issue a snappy response, *Oh really? And when were you planning to tell us?* Reeling, I managed to thank him—for nothing—and hung up the phone as if I'd dialed a wrong number.

I ran into the house, hurled myself on the bed and burrowed under the comforter, cussing like a sailor. *How could anyone be so cruel? Did he think I couldn't handle a simple no? And this is his job? When did he decide we didn't even deserve an answer?*

The doors of the Stone School had slammed shut. At the Brick School, they were still open. But Sam was drowning. I'd have to scramble to come up with an alternate plan. We had nowhere else to go. We were hanging by our fingernails. And our tuition deposit was due.

CHAPTER EIGHT

The Hottest Game in Town

When you're the parent of a well-behaved B-student with good penmanship, there's a whole educational underworld you'll never see. But when your child is flailing, people with job titles you never knew existed, come out of the woodwork.

Take Edith Goldman, the legendary education consultant: She had connections at special schools for learning differences, wilderness programs, and therapeutic boarding schools—places we never knew existed. People drove up from North Carolina to meet with her. And her office hid in plain sight, right across the street from my favorite market.

Edith Goldman was a rockstar. And she was my next, desperate hope.

I had to pull myself together. Stuart would be home late afternoon and I needed a sliver of good news to counteract the bad. I rubbed my tears, wiped my nose on my sleeve, and groped for the phone from under the covers. Dialing her number, I willed myself to stop sobbing long enough to leave a message.

Two hours later, Edith Goldman called me back. Just like that, I'd landed a coveted spot on her calendar. I found out later she held an open appointment every day for M.L.T.S. or *Mothers Losing Their Shit.*

Tomorrow would be my day. She'd see me at two o'clock sharp.

Edith Goldman would need to pull a rabbit out of her hat. By now, Sam's string of diagnoses included auditory processing problems, ADHD, learning disabilities, and a stubborn case of oppositional defiant disorder. He was hanging by a thread academically, and his school prospects had just narrowed considerably.

Who would want him? Forget whether they'd want him, who would take him?

Dr. Goldman's office was tucked above an elegant gift shop, purveyors of the trappings of domesticity and academic conformity: monogrammed Lucite trays, Florentine leather cufflink boxes, and Barbour jackets. How handy. I could pick up the perfect graduation gift for a perfect friend's perfect child on my way to figure out what was broken in my own.

I climbed the stairs to her cramped, book-lined reception area, settled nervously into a barrel-backed chair and waited.

And waited.

Behind the closed door, I heard a single muffled voice.

Then silence.

The closed door opened.

The hottest game in town looked like she'd wandered off the halls of Still Hopes, the retirement community in South Carolina where my grandfather spent his final years. At five-foot nothing, her bowl of grey hair was cut with precision. Her lined face was powdered, her lips painstakingly drawn in a jarring cherry red. I needed a hug. Instead, she extended her hand, reassuring me with her cool, authoritative handshake.

Oddly comforted, I knew I was in the right place. Somehow, I'd walk out of this office with something to move us forward.

My eyes fixed on a burley knot in the wood paneled wall as our litany of troubles spewed like steam from a pressure cooker of boiled peanuts:

Volatile marriage.

Inconsistent co-parenting.

Testing. Testing. Testing.

Attention deficit.

Ritalin.

A Go-Kart wreck.

The Stone School.

Desperation.

She raised a pen to her lips to shush me. I stammered to a stop as my face flushed. I was crossing into a manic state.

"We have six weeks," she began. "Let's look at our options."

Dr. Goldman had studied Sam's file. She knew his history, and she had a plan. "He can go back to St. Boy's, but we know that would be soul crushing. Still, with a spot in the class, it buys us some time."

She extracted a catalog from a pile on her desk and handed it to me. "I'd like to suggest this." The brochure read: Pinewood School, Charlottesville, Virginia. Did she expect us to commute two and a half hours every day? Did she want us to move? I didn't understand.

"We'd do what? Carpool?"

"It's a boarding school."

"For a ten-year-old?"

She was silent.

"I said we had options, Mrs. Harrison. I never said they'd be palatable."

My heart seized at the prospect of sending my ten-year-old to boarding school. I swallowed hard.

"This stuff is tough on families." She softened, giving me a knowing look. "Marriages, too."

———

Pinewood, a small co-ed boarding and day school, accepted children as young as fifth grade. Their specialized programs targeted Sam's very issues. But it was over an hour's drive from Richmond.

How could I begin to explain this to Stuart? He lacked the patience to turn a question over in his mind, listen to my point of view, then add his. And Sam? Would I sit down at dinner, pass the Texas toast, and a casual question, "Yo Sam. Boarding school sounds like fun, don't you think?" British royalty might ship their ten-year-olds off to school, but I couldn't fathom it for my firstborn. Not yet.

So I did nothing.

A week later, I was replaying this scene for the thousandth time when the phone rang.

"Pinewood has availability for the fall."

It was Dr. Goldman, sharing the news I'd both dreaded and hoped for.

"I'm just not ready to do that," I blurted. Soul death at St. Boy's was looking better all the time. "We've got until late September to withdraw without forfeiting tuition. If he's still struggling then, do you think Pinewood would take him?"

Dr. Goldman took a sharp breath in, but remained unflappable.

"I'll check," she said. "Oh, and Mrs. Harrison? I talked to the

Stone School."

"You did?"

"They said Sam was *highly* uncooperative in the interview."

"*Highly?* He was?"

"He told them there was no way he was going to *that* school. And he wouldn't say another word."

"I see." *Just what did they expect? Who asks a fourth-grader why he wants to change schools anyway?*

I knew we were making a mistake. Edith Goldman knew it, too. But the devil you know is better than the devil you don't know. I was still reeling from the Stone School betrayal. I didn't have the emotional stamina—not right now—to lead another charge. St. Boy's wasn't the answer. But the thought of sending Sam to Pinewood left me with a heavy heart and sick to my stomach.

Why can't my child go from fourth grade to fifth, like everybody else's? This roller coaster's gonna put me in the looney bin.

———

When Sam went back to St. Boy's that Fall, each promising day quickly turned sideways.

"Disruptive in the classroom," they noted in September, listing examples.

"He's falling behind," they added in October.

Edith Goldman wasn't just brilliant; she was clairvoyant.

By Halloween, my cop-out had unraveled. Our house reverberated with slammed doors, hurled threats, and defiant tears until finally, I broke. "Sam, honey?" I sighed as the homework battle heated up, yet again. "We just need a little space from one another, don't you think? This fussing over everything under the sun is wearing all four of us out. Your father and I found a really cool school about an hour from here that we know would be awesome for you. You'll meet a bunch of new friends and you can even ride horses with them on the weekends!"

That Sunday, we loaded Sam's camp trunk into our Suburban and the four of us climbed in for the silent drive to Charlottesville.

As we passed through Pinewood's stately entrance, Stuart shot me a look that said, *This is all your idea; it better be right.* I'd done my best to hang onto Sam, but any minute, we'd entrust him to strangers.

Set in a valley, surrounded by rolling pastures, the offices and class-rooms were in the property's original farmhouse while the dormitory, a cinderblock after-thought, was located up the hill. Inside, I surveyed a sad looking mix of "This End Up" crate furniture, chipped linoleum, and drab institutional bathrooms. How would this new "home" look through ten-year-old eyes?

I can do this.

He can do this.

I'll just pretend he's going to camp.

As I stretched a fitted sheet over the flimsy mattress on the bottom bunk, a rush of tears blinded me. I hoped my family wouldn't notice as I smoothed out the top sheet, tucked in the end and flipped up the side to make a hospital corner. This mothering touch soothed me, even if Sam might fail to notice.

As I placed neat stacks of shirts and shorts in the allotted drawers, a smiling young man with tousled hair appeared in the doorway.

"Sam! We've been waiting for you. I'm Mitch. Good to see ya, dude. I'm your dorm counselor." He patted Sam on the back then turned to greet me and Stuart. "They're ready for you in the office to go over final questions," he said in a compassionate voice, then continued brightly, "Sam and I have a busy afternoon ahead of us! You guys can talk tonight, and you'll be back to visit on Saturday, right?"

Sam looked to us for reassurance, and I nodded like a bobblehead doll. "You'll do great, buddy," said Stuart, filling the awkward moment with a good natured banter. "I'll bet they have all kinds of fun up here. And you can tell us all about it Saturday. We'll see you then."

"Okay, Sam, so I've got some guys waiting to meet you..." Mitch was a master of distraction. And as Sam turned to the three of us and waved, I knew he was putting on a brave face. We were all bracing for the amputation.

We quickly established a rhythm, going back and forth to Charlottesville most Saturdays. Once or twice a week we received reports from the teachers. The school operated like one big happy family, giving ours a respite. Without Sam's daily push and pull, Charlotte, Stuart and I settled into a shell-shocked calm. We'd been living in a state of high-alert, poised for conflict at all times. Now we could exhale, fully and deeply. Serenity began to smooth the frayed edges. I had to admit, I'd forgotten what a peaceful home felt like.

A few other Richmond children attended Pinewood. Those families, along with a couple from Charlottesville, became our support group. But, just as one wheel was tightened, another one was about to fall off.

CHAPTER NINE

An Uncivil War

Shortly before Thanksgiving, Stuart and I went on a three-day corporate retreat to an elegant resort in the mountains. Part business, part pleasure, the morning seminars left the afternoons free for tennis, golf, hiking, or spa services. Night brought cocktails and elaborate seated dinner parties. A black tie dance with a live band capped the weekend. The brokers and their spouses eagerly awaited this annual incentive trip, a reward for the firm's top producers. I, too, used to look forward to it, counting down the days. But in the weeks of relative calm at home, disturbing feelings I'd rarely had time to confront, again bubbled to the surface.

I was twenty-two when we married. Stuart and I had dated through college, so when he sprung the idea of tying the knot, it seemed like the right next thing. My mother had married young. Wasn't that what you did? I picked out a silver pattern and a June wedding date, when my grandmother assured me her prized tea roses would be in bloom.

I guess I had doubts. Doesn't every bride have *some* doubts? But once the invitations were delivered to the main post office, the toothpaste was out of the tube and I couldn't stuff it back in.

Seventeen years later, Stuart and I had become strangers. Our differences stacked up like a cord of firewood. Lacking the policy-making skills that enrich long-term relationships, we addressed each conflict superficially, if at all, and usually in a reactive mode. We had nothing to build on and no resources with which to build much of anything. We'd had blowout disagreements about Sam. And I was chasing down solutions alone, constantly lobbying for his attention, desperate for a partner.

"No time now."

"Can't you see I'm busy?"

"I've got a tee time."

"Sure we can talk. Tomorrow."

But tomorrow never came.

Stuart's attention span was short and his body language dismissive. He poured his energy into work, college football, golf, and tennis. And if I opened my mouth to speak, he'd silence me, palm-up, twelve inches from my face. Instead of resolving disagreements, he'd walk out of the room. Or the house.

Maybe I'd driven him to this point. Or maybe his mother, who'd struggled mightily with alcohol, had, in a circuitous way, taught him to build emotional walls. I no longer cared why. I was seeking solutions, survival, some warmth and fresh air. We'd dabbled at therapy, especially as Sam's problems intensified. But it was another Band-Aid and we needed a tourniquet and major surgery.

Like most Southern girls, I've often turned to country music for comfort, guidance and strength in times of trouble. Dolly, Faith and Shania have all spoken to me, saved me, in ways both cliche and profound. This time, it was Martina. I stood frozen in a department store dressing room the first time I heard "This Uncivil War." I was trying on a cocktail dress for the weekend away. I stood, unzipped, and let her words sting and chill me at once.

"There's a silence on the front lines. You can cut it with a knife."

I left the store empty handed. I needed something much more complicated than a pretty party dress.

I packed my bags for the weekend knowing that no amount of sea salt massages could change any of it. By Saturday, Stuart had spent every afternoon on the golf course. Even worse, I didn't much mind. As the sun slowly melted behind the Allegheny mountain range, my desire to pretend at a happy marriage, to present as a stylish and successful couple, waned. I stared at the evening dress hanging in the hotel closet. And in that moment, I felt a seismic shift.

I CANNOT DO THIS ANYMORE.

I wasn't putting on the dress because I was not going to the party. And I was not going to the party, because for the first time in forever, I didn't give a shit about keeping up appearances. And I didn't give a shit about keeping up appearances because, for me, our marriage had become a hollow shell. And that was my truth.

I sighed and shut the closet door. Then I pulled back the white matelasse bedspread and burrowed deep.

When I heard Stuart's key in the lock, I didn't budge. Cocktail hour would be starting soon. He had twenty minutes to shower and change. There was no time for conversation. "Why aren't you dressed?" he barked, startled to see a lump in the bed.

"I'm not going," I managed, quiet on the outside, but top-of-my-lungs inside. I'd closed that closet door ever-so-gently, but it was my first real roar. He dressed in a hurry and left the room, shaking his head in disbelief. I fell into a deep sleep, exhausted from the energy it took to find my voice.

You can stay and take your chances.

Or you can run to save your life.

One side is retreating.

And the other's runnin' scared.

Martina must have a telescope into our relationship.

Do I stay with what I know? We'd been together seventeen years. But it's dark in here, and cramped. And I'm claustrophobic. *Should I throw in the towel?* This relationship is unhealthy for all of us; maybe we'd work better together if we lived apart.

———

Sunday afternoon as we drove home in silence, it was crystal clear I'd fought my last internal war. Reba McEntire's new hit, *Lonely Alone,* came on the radio, another message from the Country Goddesses.

Somewhere around Staunton, I broke the silence.

"Stuart, neither one of us has been happy for a long time."

His jaw tightened. Eyes on the road.

"And I can't do this anymore. I've decided. I'm sorry."

He let out a sigh, slapped on his sunglasses and we rode home in more silence.

My whole life had been about following the rules, doing the right thing. And suddenly, not only had I spoken my truth, but I felt sure I'd scrape together the courage to live it, too. It felt like jumping out of a plane, with nothing but faith that my parachute would go *flooph!* and blow up like a giant mushroom before I crashed to the ground. I don't know what came over me, but I no longer gave a flying flip what anyone thought. And I prayed doubly hard that our children would one day understand.

"You've lived so long under a rock," a friend later told me, "you're used to the darkness. Sunshine feels good, but it'll be blinding at first. You're getting the freedom and clarity you crave, but it's fraught with uncertainty." She was right. But once I stepped out of that dark, cramped place, I craved more and more light.

In the quiet little places, you can see the little faces.

Huddled right outside the bedroom door.

Praying for an end to this uncivil war.

Martina and I spent a lot of time praying.

With our marriage strained beyond recognition, Stuart agreed we needed to separate. The day we told our children was devastating—for all four of us. Sam was home for the weekend, so we gathered as a family. He burst into tears and stomped upstairs to his room, slamming the door so hard that the family room blinds slapped against the window frame. Charlotte sat between us, hands folded on her lap, and stared straight ahead. Quiet as a mouse.

Stuart moved out of our house and into his apartment the week of my fortieth birthday. It wasn't how I'd pictured it, as celebrations go.

CHAPTER TEN

Dirty Work

When my children were young, I worked the front lines.

Field trip?

My car holds six.

Room mother?

Dues by the 15th, please.

Costumes for the third-grade play? International tasting day?

Bet your borscht, I'll dust off my Singer.

I embraced the full-time mother job. But I fully expected to go back to work once my children were settled in school. I'd studied accounting, majored in business, and before I had Sam I'd worked, briefly, for the law firm with the porcelain bus on the fourth floor. I'd been hired by the best. I'd shared an office. I had business cards. And I was earning corporate respect. Short-lived as it was, my position as a recruiting coordinator fed a hunger to use my brain. I loved the work, the people, the thinking.

Once I was separated and my head was bobbing above water again, that craving returned with growling pangs. But this time it was my soul that longed to be fed. Working with my hands in the soil and nurturing plants had been therapy the last several years. I vowed my next job would cultivate my creative talents. If only I knew what those were.

The answer, it turned out, was as plain as the dirt under my fingernails.

I lived in a part of town where women cut roses, not grass. But our street was different. Six of us worked tirelessly in our gardens—some proudly pushing lawn mowers. While our children wheeled around on bikes, shot driveway baskets or played make-believe in backyard play-houses, we planted bulbs, pored over seed catalogs, and debated the merits of lace cap hydrangeas over mop heads. Our shared passion inspired each of us to dig deeper and, over time, a connection snaked around us like wisteria, growing steadfast and strong.

A green thumb ran on both sides of my family. My maternal grand-parents grew prize roses, and my father's father farmed corn and soy-beans. One spring, as I watched my Spanish bluebells and quince erupt in a riot of color, an idea sprouted inside of me. *I can do this.*

With Sam tucked away at school and Stuart moved out, I wasn't holding my breath anymore. My oxygenated lungs restored my spirit and creativity started to bloom. I didn't realize how much pain I'd been suppressing, how buttoned up I'd been, how the relationship had drained me. In those first few months of separation, I unfurled like a flower after a much needed spring rain. A new message flickered in my mind: *It's time. And I'm ready.*

———

My neighbor, Annie, had just earned her Landscape Design Certification through George Washington University. I was thrilled to learn that the

D.C. school offered satellite classes in Richmond. Now that I'd traded diapers and sandboxes for baseball and ballet, I craved a creative and intellectual challenge. I didn't miss the pumps and pantyhose, but the mothers who showed up for teacher conferences in business suits reminded me that I longed for work of my own—and a paycheck. Maybe I could turn my gardening passion into a business. I'd wear boots and jeans, dig in the dirt, and get paid for it! Annie had three children and if she could do it, why couldn't I?

When I registered for the program, I couldn't wait to dive in. I headed straight downtown to Main Art with my supply list: colored pencils, notebooks, a drafting table, T-square, graph paper, vellum overlays, and Michael Dirr's, *Manual of Woody Landscape Plants*.

Wandering the aisles, I racked my brain for ways to buy study time. I'd order pizza two nights a week, arrange for backup carpool, cook ahead and freeze some meals. Charlotte was ready for some "big girl" chores. This would be good for her, too.

I set up the drafting table near the picture window in my bedroom. I'd planned everything—the class days, the schedules; Charlotte could stay at Stuart's when I had project deadlines. I imagined myself inspired and productive and successful. By this time next year, my client list would be a country mile long.

———

Stuart and I continued to exchange prickly communications through our lawyers. We'd attempted mediation, in an effort to keep costs down and adversity at a minimum. That did not prove to be successful—at all—and I had to seek my own representation. After months of discussion and negotiation, our separation agreement specified that we sell our house where I still lived. I started the landscape design program with my house on the market.

"A neighborhood like this?" said my realtor Eleanor Hines Custis, through her pack-a-day rasp. "It'll sell in a heartbeat, you'll see." But keeping a house market-ready wasn't easy. Each time Eleanor held a showing, I dismantled my drafting table and stowed it out of sight.

———

At twelve, Sam was now bigger than me, a hulking man-child whose moodiness was spiked with aggression. I walked on eggshells, afraid of setting him off. And the cherry on top? He cussed like a sailor.

Summer was fast approaching and Sam required constant supervision when he was home. Camp wasn't an option. How would I manage him? If I answered the phone or focused on a project for even a minute, I'd find him revving his go-cart into the busy street, slamming his skateboard over an unwieldy ramp, or simply missing.

That fall, Sam would enter his second—and last—year at Pinewood. I was frantic. Where would I find his next school?

———

In class, I was transported to a place I'd been craving deep in my bones. The idea of dreaming up beautiful swaths of blooms and mapping out the design with precision and a T-square lit me up from the inside. But the hours of homework choked me, sapping my energy. I'd stay up into the wee hours just to keep up with the barrage of assignments.

Eleanor was right; we got a contract on our house within days. So now, I turned my attention to house hunting. I quickly settled on a Tudor style, listed "as is" and priced just right, but sorely in need of an A-Z makeover. I imagined the new bathrooms, stainless appliances, and bleached floorboards and did what every homebuyer does: I underestimated the time, money, and energy I'd need to get the renovation project done.

Charlotte and I moved into a tiny rental house where, to avoid paying for a storage unit, I stuffed our extra furniture onto a screen porch we'd never use. Barely keeping up in class, my projects were half-assed at best. My father would call this *cramming two pounds of horse-shit in a one pound bag*. Looking back, I'd call it insanity.

———

When it came to Sam, I'd assumed the unofficial role of scout, pricking up my ears, listening out for the expert who could untangle his collection of growing challenges. Edith Goldman was a Godsend when it came to finding schools. But I continued scanning the horizon for the special specialist who could manage his whole bag of tricks. So far, the support I'd found had been piecemeal; a tutor for this, a diagnostic for that. He'd see an audiologist or a therapist, then wash it all down with a prescription. I'd find a specialist, beg Stuart to remember the appointment, haul Sam home from Pinewood, if needed. But after our allotted fifty minutes, Sam's file would go back in the drawer, and we'd be out on our butt in the snow. Couldn't one of these specialists just move in with us? There were no easy answers.

Uncomfortable in his own skin, Sam was restless, edgy and frustrated, his mind never still long enough to allow him to focus. Once I understood this core truth about my ADHD child, how the disorder prevented him from slowing the whirligig in his mind and and drawing on his inner resources, I stopped wanting to throttle him, wanting to weep for him, instead.

He wouldn't "grow out of it." Not now. Sam's emotional, behavioral, and social problems would follow him into adulthood unless we intervened. I'd heard through the neighborhood grapevine about Edward Brooks, a specialist who'd treated many of Virginia's most challenging children. Boys mostly. Rebellious, oppositional, sent-to-the-office, ADHD boys. Mine was all of the above.

His treatment involved forming an integrated team, the brochure explained, "to help patients recognize their strengths in all five of life's major performance areas: medical, emotional, educational, vocational, and social." I made a desperate call to Brooks. From what I'd heard, Sam would be treated as a whole person, not a grab-bag of symptoms.

Teasing out a true disorder from the tangle of normal adolescent pitfalls is an inexact science. Moods shift, depression rolls in like storm clouds, hormones ebb and flow, spiking anxiety, even for the most well-adjusted teens. The only pattern is that there is no pattern.

No single person can save your child. It takes an army.

When Edward Brooks agreed to see me, I wanted to fall to my knees in gratitude. If I'd tried to translate the information I'd gathered for Stuart, he might readily dismiss it. I was banking on the premise that when wisdom comes from an expert, it's usually more palatable. I found myself humming *Amazing Grace* as I pulled into a parking space behind a low slung white office building on the south side of town. As I locked the car door, I braced myself.

Here we go again.

I can do this.

The waiting room was lined with photos of boys looking carefree and fit. They wore backpacks and hiking boots. They rock climbed, kayaked, rappelled. Dr. Brooks had pioneered a wilderness therapy program, and I imagined Sam's face in those group shots, another one of Brooks' success stories.

He opened the door and ushered me into his office. The bookcase displayed duck decoys, climbing ropes, carabiners, a pick axe. Sitting across from him, the monologue I'd delivered to Dr. Goldman years earlier tumbled out of my mouth, accelerated by more anxiety. *Will I ever be able to stop telling this story?* Dr. Brooks listened intently. *Would there ever be a happy ending?*

"You've got a constellation of issues at work here," he explained. "Learning issues, oppositional defiance, two parents who aren't on the same page. So our solution needs to be multifaceted—just like the problem. Otherwise, we're fixing one hand on the clock."

Hallelujah! For the first time, the shrink behind the big desk would look at Sam holistically—lining up the academic, behavioral, emotional, and family issues and how they work in concert. *This won't be easy, but I'm ready to dig in again. We're finally in the right place now. Thank God. If only I can get Stuart on board.*

Testing would be the first order of business, Dr. Brooks explained. "To establish an academic baseline." Counseling would cover every combination of relationships among the three of us: Sam to Sam, Sam to Stuart, Sam to me, Sam to Stuart and me. Brooks was covering all bases. He promised to add Charlotte to the mix in due time. Wilderness programs were a possibility, he added. And, if necessary, we'd explore a therapeutic boarding school. The kind where therapy is dished out alongside math and history assignments.

I left that day with a sense of hope, taking warped comfort in the knowledge that Sam's problems were real and far more pervasive than I had realized. I wasn't the only mother trying to work a puzzle without the picture. Brooks had seen boys like Sam before. And he'd fixed them, as the photos in his waiting room attested.

I drove home feeling upbeat, ready to get back to the drafting table. We had an ace on the case. I also felt validated. I wasn't imagining Sam's problems, wasn't micromanaging him, or saddling my rambunctious juvenile with unrealistic expectations.

For this window of time, Dr. Brooks would be our Commander-in-Chief.

———

"You've got that kid under a microscope," Stuart had griped more than once. *Did I?* Other boys his age could rattle off college baseball stats, fish for hours from the banks of the James, or wheel a golf bag over eighteen holes. But Sam lacked the internal mechanism to lose himself in a goal or a passion. Like a bicycle with a loose chain, he couldn't grab hold, engage, and activate his own reservoir of talents; so they remained untapped.

"People with ADD know two kinds of time," says Ned Hallowell, author of the groundbreaking book, *Driven to Distraction*. "There's now and there's not-now." The line always gets a big laugh from parents, but the upshot is tragic. What's missing, of course, is the extended now—the hours invested in nurturing a new skill, whether it's tying flies or hitting a backhand. For Sam, that could mean teaching Bo, his golden retriever, to duck hunt. But the ADHD kid can't abide the wait. He needs instant gratification or he's off chasing the next shiny object. And that was my Sam.

My visit with Dr. Brooks confirmed that something was not right, the belief I'd held long before I lost my religion on Roslyn Road.

———

In the mid '90s, issues like Sam's were just coming to light, like the field of adolescent psychiatry itself. It was, however, a dark subject, not openly discussed outside of clinical or academic settings. Back then, the word psychiatry still brought to mind a "cuckoo's nest" of padded cells, strait-jackets, and lobotomy scars. I was so clueless about the study of behavioral health that when I'd heard my Denver friend Susan was studying psychiatry, I wondered what kind of nut jobs would wind up on her client list. A psychiatrist was for other people. Not me. Not *my* family.

By some miracle, Stuart reluctantly agreed to meet at Dr. Brooks' office the following week. I rescheduled the floor sander and got an extension on the latest homework assignment.

Dr. Brooks outlined his strategy. Treating Sam would involve a psychologist, a behavioral modification therapist, a this, a that. And lots of money. His plan would require work on Stuart's part, my part. Sam's rules and routines would need to remain consistent between our two households. We needed an all-hands-on-deck approach and a blank check to go with it. "And," Dr. Brooks added with caution, "we still have no guarantees that our efforts will pay off. Sam has to meet us halfway."

Stuart listened half-heartedly, glancing at his watch and fidgeting as if he had more important things to do. I knew what was coming. Quiet and polite, until we stepped out the front door of Dr Brooks' office, he threw up his hands in opposition and spewed, "This is a *fucking racket!*"

as he turned and stormed off to his car.

The words stung like a cold slap. With one sweeping insult, he'd dismissed my scouting, research, maternal judgment, and finely-tuned instincts. I stood in the parking lot feeling utterly alone as he backed his car out of the space and drove off. I'd been laying the groundwork for this meeting for months and, in an instant, he'd thrown up a roadblock.

I had no idea how I'd negotiate this curveball. It was a stretch for Stuart to set foot in a psychiatrist's office. Maybe he'd been overwhelmed by Brooks' unvarnished approach. Maybe his anger and opposition, which looked a lot like arrogance to me, was sheer terror? I'd taken comfort in Brooks' step-by-step strategy, but, for Stuart, Brooks was a complete stranger who was proposing a colossal, confusing time-suck with an uncertain payoff. Twenty years of distance has helped me see this watershed moment through Sam's father's eyes.

Over the next six weeks, we returned to Brooks' office to study test scores, review graphs, and answer exhaustive questions: *Does Sam have a curfew? (Yes and no.) What were our communication styles? (There are styles?) Our trigger subjects? (All of the above?)* I'd remind Stuart of these appointments over and over, but they never ranked high on his priority list. More than once he'd "forget" or something would "come up at work."

We were lifting the lid on Pandora's Box, terrified of what we'd find inside. Each week, the information Dr. Brooks gathered on Sam became more dense. We were in deep, and Stuart and I had to put more skin in the game. This wasn't like dropping Sam off for a tutoring session. We both needed to show up and commit. To answer the hard questions, we needed to get in touch with our day to day dilemmas. But the deeper Dr. Brooks probed, the more impatient and dismissive Stuart became. Meanwhile, I was falling desperately behind in class.

"When can we meet next week?" Dr. Brooks inquired, as we wrapped up our fifth meeting.

"I've got class on Tuesday and Thursday," I said, paging through my dog-eared appointment book, but I'm free any other time."

"I've got back-to-back appointments next week. I don't know what to tell you," Stuart said, looking my way, shoulders shrugged.

Dr. Brooks stiffened. Slowly pulling his glasses from his nose, he dropped them on the coffee table between us, sighed deeply, then spoke gingerly, choosing each word with great care.

"What works best, Mr. and Mrs. Harrison, is when the families with whom we are working are on board with our protocol. Our goal is to create a lifelong game plan for this young man. And if we can't get off the starting block, I see this relationship," he made a looping gesture from his chest to us and back, "as being unproductive."

My heart broke again. *Was Dr. Brooks firing us?* We weren't seeing king-sized results just yet, but I felt certain he was putting us on a path that could help Sam and our whole family.

I was devastated. In retrospect, I guess Dr. Brooks' policy was merciful. He could have kept us coming, taken our money indefinitely. But he knew he couldn't help us—or Sam—as long as we weren't aligned. And maybe Stuart was equally merciful, because he had no intention of adopting Dr. Brooks' all-consuming plan. He'd made that perfectly clear on the very first day.

I came home to my rental house that afternoon feeling battered. The refinished floors in the new house didn't dry on schedule, forcing me to extend our move-in date. We were still living out of boxes and I'd missed two classes and fumbled a project deadline. I'd worked every free minute, often late into the night, whenever Charlotte stayed with her dad. Still, I never caught up. Let's just say there wasn't time to sit back and smell the hyacinths, much less learn their Latin names. I was always behind the eight ball and now Dr. Brooks was firing us. This was the last straw.

I was forced to put my garden dreams on the back burner. I dropped out of the landscape design program. The failure left me empty and deflated. Would I ever have anything that I could call *my own*? I pictured tires spinning in a snowbank. Would I ever take hold of the solid ground I needed to move forward?

I'd hear the grandparents admonish and shake their heads wistfully: *They grow up so fast. You don't want to miss it. You have a responsibility to put your children first, while they're young.* Maybe it wasn't my time yet. The excitement the class had sparked was fading. And in the background, I could hear the Career Gods mocking me:

You want to develop your authentic self?

You want to crackle with purpose and accomplishment?

You dream of finding your passion and getting paid for it, too?

We'll just see about that.

In the years to come, I would call Edith Goldman again and again. Sam would see over a dozen experts and accumulate a string of new diagnoses: Bipolar Disorder with episodes of Grandiosity, Borderline Personality Disorder, and Narcissistic Personality Disorder. I lost count.

The road seemed endless, grueling and undefined. The only way I'd get through was to pick up one snow boot at a time.

Dr. Brooks had thrown us a lifeline, but before he could pull us to safety, Stuart had cut us loose. Now, I treaded water, alone in a dark ocean, as the rescue ship sailed away. I watched as it got smaller and smaller until finally, it disappeared on the horizon.

CHAPTER ELEVEN

The Times We Never Had

I'd pinned my hopes on Edward Brooks and, now that he'd fired us, I had no backup plan. No next step, I floated through the days ahead, numb and hopeless. "How long have we been doing this?" I pleaded to Lang, when I called to tell her. "It's not getting any easier."

As second grade had turned into third, then to sixth and seventh, a sad reality was emerging: It wasn't only what was happening to Sam that was heartbreaking, it was also what *wasn't.*

"I wish I could tell you how Sam sank the winning basket in the middle-school playoffs or led the Easter procession at church. I'd like to think he watched the sunrise while sitting—patiently, I might add—in a duck blind with his grandfather," I rattled on, as if to myself.

"You can't," Lang said knowingly. "Because he didn't."

In the places where life was supposed to unfold into happy snapshots and memories, Sam only had blank spaces. The honorable mentions. The good-conduct stars. The homework paper with a check plus or "great job" written on top. Those went home in other children's backpacks and were affixed with magnets to other refrigerators in other houses belonging to other parents.

There were no school dances. No team rosters. No college tours. And later, no visits to a studio apartment, rented excitedly after he'd graduated and landed his first real job.

I brought it up in Book Club, the next time we met, and all around the room, heads nodded at the birthday cakes unlit and family trips untraveled.

"The times we never had," Lang clucked from her perch around Celeste's coffee table. "I've got a list of happy family memories that were never made. We all do."

———

From the moment we start dreaming of a family, we create a set of expectations. But if the budding quarterback you'd imagined turns out to be a math-lete, you recalculate your route toward this new destination. And, you'll get there eventually. Both of you.

With addiction, it's different. It tiptoes in on little cat feet and cunningly rearranges your hopes and dreams. Parents stand by helplessly while a son or daughter is sucked into its vortex. A beer here leads to a bong hit there. And once it's up and running, addiction robs us, and them, of their youth. The child we knew is swept away, overwhelmed by this ugly intruder.

How do we prepare? Pay close attention. Trust your gut. When your bubbly cheerleader holes up in her room trading dark poetry in furtive chat rooms, the handwriting's on the wall. It's out of character. It doesn't jive. Get involved.

———

The most merciful friends are the ones who look out for you when you're single. I was lucky that mine were willing to play matchmaker. A divorced, insurance executive, Robert lived on Philadelphia's Main Line, while raising his two sons. A hometown boy, he returned to Richmond every few months to visit his parents. On one of those visits, we ventured out on a blind date that went mercifully right.

He charmed me with his dimples and dry sense of humor. Over dinner, we discovered dozens of mutual friends. I wasn't emotionally equipped for a full-time relationship, so Robert's distance felt right. I'd see him when he was in town. And in the meantime, we'd talk on the phone late into the night, as our friendship grew into something more.

With Robert's business world in Philadelphia and his sons firmly entrenched in school there, we'd continued our long-distance relationship. We sealed the deal one February, with family and a few close friends as witnesses. Our separate home bases kept family upheaval to a minimum, we reasoned. Once everybody left for college, we would buy or build a house of our own, a shared nest.

In the meantime, we tended our own children from our respective cities during the week. On the weekends, we burned up I-95, sometimes with those children in tow. The shift was so gradual, we joked, maybe they wouldn't even notice.

When families are blended by remarriage, issues that were once yours or mine become ours. The child with the "substance-abuse problem" is a pre-existing condition, like diabetes or asthma, adding a layer of stress to an already challenging family dynamic. The ups and downs of addiction are rarely convenient, so step-parents struggle to supply the megadoses of empathy routinely required of them.

"Those times you never have keep adding up," Celeste had warned us that night at Book Club. "And they'll follow you."

Robert and I were at a football game in Charlottesville five years later, when I fell into an indignant funk. I was fighting back tears at the tailgate picnic. The stadium was abuzz under a pristine, blue October sky. The band was playing, the crowd was cheering, and halfway across the country, Sam was sitting in a jail cell. Celeste was right. I was being followed. By another one of the times I hadn't had.

"What's up with you?" Robert grumbled, taking my funk personally. *Who could be unhappy on a gorgeous day like this?* Was that what he was thinking? A sleeping Ursula the Sea Witch suddenly spiraled up from the deep. "Are you f-ing kidding me?" I hissed. I almost snatched him bald-headed. "Here I am at *The* University of Virginia with everybody else's college-aged child but mine."

"You're here with your step-son?" he ventured, throwing spaghetti against the tailgate, hoping it would stick.

"I know, but I've never shared this experience with Sam. You can't know what it's like." By now, my top lip was quivering uncontrollably and tears were ruining my eyeliner. "It's sad, that's all. Let me have my pity-party, pleeeeeaaase?"

"This isn't new, Lynda," he pressed. "We've been dealing with this for a long time." He was stepping into danger zone. "Why now?"

"I have no earthly idea. Just leave me alone. Let me sit in my own shit for a while. They're my feelings and I'm entitled to them. Give me some time. It'll pass. It usually does."

He threw his hands in the air and muttered, "Got it." As he walked away, I could tell he was grappling with a new level of compassion, trying to understand my feelings— even when they didn't make complete sense to me, either. My husband could not fathom the devastation I felt in that moment. No one could for that matter, unless they had experience on the front lines.

My sinking spell wasn't only because Sam sat in a Colorado jail on that crisp, fall football Saturday. It was about the picture of him I'd carried in my head all these years.

In it, Sam's just another college kid, cheering his team from the bleachers. *Was that too much to ask?* Clearly, I had some reframing to do.

———

My newest Book Club friend, Cece, calls it the parenting paycheck. That rush of satisfaction you feel when your child makes you proud, when you glimpse a little payoff. But when your child is an ongoing source of frustration and fear, you start comparing notes. You think, *I never signed up for this job.*

We were having lunch at my favorite salad spot when Cece put this feeling into words: "In eighteen years, there was absolutely nothing we could be proud of," she said, liberated by the confession. "I didn't realize how desperately I needed that positive reinforcement. Who doesn't? Just throw me a bone, kid?" By now she's starting to laugh at her own petty wish. "Give me a homework paper that says *Good Job!* or a Brown Ribbon at the science fair."

"There's a brown ribbon? Seriously?"

"Eighth place. We'll take it! That's the parenting paycheck. The A-okay sign," Cece explained. "So your child's not a frontrunner. But he's in the pack, dammit."

Cece sighed. "My older brothers were geniuses. One went to Dartmouth. One graduated Phi Beta Kappa. That was my norm. So now I've landed in an upside-down world. My son's at the bottom of the class, propped up by a parade of tutors. I don't know this world. I've got to get my bearings. And poor Nate. I love my son to pieces but we've never had one moment when our hearts swelled with pride." She caught her breath, looking down. This regret felt small-minded and selfish. "Oh wait. I take that back. There was one time."

"You had one?" I sure as hell hadn't.

"Second grade. A laminated card came home from school in his backpack. It was a green circle that said *I had a GOOD DAY today!*"

CHAPTER TWELVE

I Couldn't Find the Zipper

Without a drafting table and deadlines, I'd created some "white space" on the calendar, time to exhale.

Charlotte, now eight, and I headed to South Carolina for the weekend. Two girls, hitting the road for a little grandparent time. We planned to watch Florida State play Clemson in the Tigers' Death Valley stadium. We'd be greeted with tailgates, swaths of orange and purple, and loads of old friends. Everyone would be there. But what should have been a care-free social weekend ended with a trip to the emergency room and a prescription for a dozen Xanax, shaped just like little orange footballs.

I was in my childhood bedroom when I woke up Sunday morning, my mind racing. I knew something was *bad* wrong. Charlotte was sleeping soundly next to me. Holding my breath, I slid out of bed and tiptoed downstairs, praying that a warm cup of tea might steady me. As I put the water on to boil, I was talking and talking and talking—to myself. I could not complete a sentence. I couldn't even figure out what I was trying to say.

My thoughts skittered like marbles on glass. Nothing I did—deep breaths, closing my eyes, placing my head between my knees—could slow the scattered, fast moving fragments. I come from a family of talkers. We sit at the dinner table long after dessert, rehashing hometown news from every angle. Any minute, my parents would appear at the kitchen door, eager to fire up the conversation over coffee. Normally, I'd find this comforting. But the harder I tried to collect myself, the more agitated I became.

Was I sick? Was this an emergency?

I felt confined. Claustrophobic—a recurring theme. Antsy. I wanted to crawl out of my skin, but I couldn't find the zipper. And I couldn't shake thoughts of Roslyn Road, the day I lost control, flooded by undefined emotion. *Was it happening again—in a different way?*

I'd been burning the candle at both ends for months, like an adrenaline junkie, running faster and faster, just to show the world that I was A-okay, thank you very much. My body hadn't recovered from the chronic stress of separation, moving, and Sam's shenanigans. I was ready to move my life forward, determined to appear invincible. But my body was holding me back.

How would I fake cool, calm, and collected around my daughter? How could I possibly *drive* back to Richmond?

My mother came downstairs first, took one look at me and knew something was off. When my father appeared in his bathrobe, the two exchanged a vigilant look and kicked into gear.

After waffling back and forth, they agreed that my dad would drive me to the ER while my mother stayed behind with Charlotte who, by now, was sitting in front of the television in a sleepy stupor, distracted by cartoons and cereal.

In the waiting room, I tried to reassure my worried father but couldn't pin down the words. My friend Amelia had opened a sleek new yoga studio, and I focused on my breath, like she taught in class. Still my thoughts whirled, caught in a blender.

Over the past several months, I'd worked so hard to appear okay that I had nothing left in reserve, nothing saved up for an emergency. The familiarity of this blender feeling made it all the more terrifying.

Given the choice, I would have preferred a compound fracture of the femur complete with six months of traction. Instead, this problem was inside of me. *I* was the injury.

When they ushered me into the exam room, I flushed with embarrassment. How could I explain what was wrong?

"Have you been under stress lately?" asked the fluffy nurse in a repetitive, saccharine voice. *Who me? Under stress? Like if a piano fell on my head from a third floor window? Hell yeah,* I wanted to scream as I took in her teddy-bear-scrubs-over-Crocs ensemble. *What was your first clue, Nancy Drew?* Instead. I offered her a weak, "Sorta."

The doctor appeared in short order, distracted and weary, as he read from a clipboard. After ruling out heart-attack, acid indigestion, stroke, and Morton's neuroma, he announced his diagnosis: Anxiety with a capital A.

How could a *feeling* land you in the emergency room, I wondered? Like dying of embarrassment, it seemed far fetched.

"Take these," he said, as the nurse handed him a sample-pack of anti-anxiety medication she'd found in the cabinet. "You'll want to follow up with your psychiatrist when you get back to Virginia."

My psychiatrist? I'd never seen a psychiatrist—about myself. I only knew of one. Period.

"Don't worry," the nurse smiled sweetly, changing her tone and slipping me an extra sample-pack after the doctor left the room. "We see this a lot on Sundays."

Back at my parents' house, I dialed Richmond. "This isn't about Sam," I whimpered to Dr. Brooks' emergency answering machine, "But can you help me? I don't know who else to call. Please? I'm paralyzed."

He returned my call first thing the next morning, agreeing to work me in on Tuesday, but insisting I find someone to drive me home from South Carolina. The driver-part was a no-brainer. My mother volunteered. When we left on Monday, mid-morning, Charlotte rode in front while I curled into a pillow and blanket on the back seat. I practiced looking out of my *third eye*, the gate to higher consciousness, and slipped in and out of sleep during the six and a half hour trip home. I imagined myself finding safety but couldn't fathom what it would look like.

CHAPTER THIRTEEN
Cashmere and Compassion

"Sistah, you need to get yourself some help!" my friend Amelia told me, as I pieced together the story of what I'd now learned was my first full-blown panic attack.

"Amelia, I was walking in circles, I couldn't breathe. I couldn't think straight."

"You need to see Pat Buxton. I'll let her know you'll be calling."

"I need help?" I balked. Compared to Stuart and Sam, wasn't I the one holding it all together?

"They're doing this to me! *They* need the help."

"You ain't gonna change them, Sistah, you can only change how you respond to whatever is thrown your way. Grab a pen and write this number down."

I opened my palm and scribbled on it, illegibly, like an first-grader.

"Oh and Lynda?" Amelia paused the way she does when she's not fooling around.

"She's not like the others."

———

"Let me get this straight," Pat said holding up both hands, deflecting my avalanche. "You quit your landscaping class because you cancelled the floor sander and got fired by Edward Brooks. And the furniture's stacked on the screen porch? In boxes?"

I hadn't even gotten to the part about the wilderness program. Sam had finished Pinewood. In the wake of the Brooks debacle, and per Edith Goldman's latest recommendation, we had all piled in the car two weeks later and headed to his next stop, Elkin Academy, a wilderness program in the backwoods of West Virginia that promised equal parts Algebra, English, climbing and discipline. Sam had always loved climbing. I'd found him on top of the refrigerator more than a few times when he was young. So I focused on the climbing component and tried to sell it to Sam as one big jungle gym of a school.

Even though I feared the turnaround was too quick for him, it had seemed like an answer to my prayers. He would take to the streets, roaming who-knows-where for hours at a time. When he did come home, he was full of rage at worst and grumpy at best. His moods ricocheted from irritable to angry to hostile. The promise of an outdoor school seemed to make sense.

At the same time, the idea of sending my wanderer into the wild had terrified me. What if they didn't keep track of him like I did? What if Sam started roaming and just kept going? What if I never saw him again? I forced myself to ignore my fears—even though I'm convinced many of them were quite rational. I told myself that not only could Sam handle it, he required it. Charlotte and I needed it, too.

We were settling into our new house, but it hadn't been easy. With

Sam's erratic behavior in the mix, our bumpy ride had gone off road. We needed Sam to land in the right place again—and to land on his feet. We were hoping the great outdoors of West Virginia would be the solution. I took a deep breath, realizing I was lost in thought and anxiety. She cocked her head, incredulous. "And then a football game put you in the ER?"

———

I'd arrived with list in hand, ready to lay out my history in crisp order, crisis by crisis. But once she fixed her gaze on me, my pain unspooled in a loopy run-on sentence:

"My tuition refund was being processed.

I had to drop the program.

I wanted to sink heart-and-soul into garden design.

And my parents had preached stick-to-it-ive-ness.

I hated scrapping my plans and dropping this credit would screw up my whole schedule."

I sucked some air into my lungs and continued:

"We had to find another school.

Edward Brooks was great, but he fired us;

So Sam started smoking pot

and the residential advisor called a conference;

and my drafting table was packed up for the move,

so I couldn't finish my homework.

I was so gonna nail that assignment.

Spring perennial borders.

Cool colors.

I had the colored pencils.

The parallel bar.

The vellum overlays.

I was in the zone, Pat.

And Charlotte was going with Stuart that weekend. Right?

But then it all unraveled.

And I'm supposed to drive to God-forsaken West Virginia to put out another fire.

I just can't get any freaking traction.

How can I memorize the Latin names of indigenous plants?

Tell me. How?

When my family's in a tailspin?

I've also got Charlotte.

She's eight, and absorbing all this stress!"

This was my first visit to the office of Pat Buxton, MA, MSW, board certified Alexander Technique teacher and, already, she was getting more than she bargained for. She'd greeted me like an old friend and motioned for me to sit down. Settling into her chair, she slid open an elegant box, struck a wooden match and lit the votive candle on her desk. *Thank God, I have two hours in this first session to download.* We'd need every minute.

"Tell me why you're here today," she said, pointing to a tilted footrest under my chair. Pat is certified in the *Alexander Technique*, which teaches that our mental stress is connected to our physical tension. Athletes, singers, dancers, musicians—and harried parents like me—use the process to control their skeletal and muscular posture and habitual reactions to stress. Pat teaches that proper body alignment heightens self-awareness, and that the technique is a way of learning how to move mindfully through life. No more than a hundred and five pounds soaking wet, she was fine-boned and dressed in beige cashmere. She carried herself with the soft, fluid movement of a dancer.

I took a breath and steadied myself. I had what appeared to be a lifetime of turmoil bottled up inside and the cork was about to blow. I couldn't help myself; I wanted to tell her everything all at once.

"Okay," Pat clasped her hands like she'd just caught a lighting bug, "Let's hold those thoughts." She radiated serenity and I let out a staccato exhale. Surely, she could help me corral the wild horses trampling my left brain, like Edith Goldman had attempted to do when she shushed my Stone School diatribe.

"Here's how I work," she articulated. "It's a little different from traditional therapy."

Pat explained that this wasn't about my son.

Or my daughter.

Or their father.

Not just yet.

We weren't here to analyze my childhood,

my passion for camellias,

or my high school boyfriend.

Not today.

Our work, she went on, was about how I responded to what was happening right under my nose.

"Right here," she said.

I squirmed in my chair.

"Right now."

She folded her arms and serenely sat. And sat.

Holy shit. I want to be this woman when I grow up.

I'd heard about codependence before but had never stopped to think that I might need to better acquaint myself with its meaning. Until then.

Pat's definition went something like this: You put your own needs on the back burner and busy yourself taking care of someone else's needs.

The healthy version of helping someone looks like a simple gesture of kindness, say, dropping off homemade soup for a friend who's sick with the flu. When codependence enters the picture, things get wonky; you move in with that friend, stock her freezer with homemade casseroles, clean her shower grout with a Q-tip, then wash and iron all of her family's laundry. The thank-yous are intoxicating. Your own needs pale in comparison. A week or so isn't enough. Oh no. You keep this going until you've lost your job, your car's been repossessed and your house is in foreclosure. Because, you rationalize, you're such a giver.

At the heart of codependence, boundaries define the point at which we end and the other person begins. And other people are all too happy to encroach, trampling them and forcing us to grow a backbone to hold the line. Pat assessed my boundaries and found them decidedly lacking. One gust of wind and, like a house of straw, poof! the boundary walls are blown over.

Imagine eating dinner with a friend who picks up her fork and pokes around on your plate, tasting. Or the close-talker who backs you across the room at a cocktail party, carrying on a conversation while intruding on your personal space. These are boundary violations. And we can either hand over our dinner and get backed into a wall, or we can politely stand our ground.

"But what happens when the people violating my boundaries are my own children? Or their father?"

"Family?" Pat shrugged, "They're often the primary offenders."

When you ignore your own needs to tend to someone else's, you create a negative loop that, over time, plays in your head:

How can you be so selfish at a time like this?

Somebody else is in crisis, and they need you.

You can't possibly [start that job] [have that hysterectomy] [take that class] [slip out for a ten minute brow wax] while so-and-so is dealing with [fill in the problem]. Better put your own needs aside, for the moment. Or forever.

With Sam, the crisis was rarely over. And my negative loop was playing, round the clock, in stereo, high-fidelity, surround-sound. He wasn't deliberately bungling each new school, Pat surmised, but our rescues had taught him that we'd jump through hoops to ensure another school awaited, after each new catastrophe.

My responses to other people's problems had been involuntary, like breathing or swallowing. I didn't know anything else. But once I raised my level of awareness, I should be able to respond from a place of clarity and consciousness.

"You do have choices about how you respond," Pat insisted.

I couldn't see my choices yet, but if Pat said I had them, I believed her.

"So we'll start right here," Pat sliced the air with her hand, then pushed it forward. "The opposite of codependence is independence. But that's a skill-set few of us are given in our youth. We're taught to drive. We make up our bed every morning, scrub our bathroom once a week. We manage our first checking account. But, sometimes, emotional independence isn't in the family curriculum. So to get to independence, we're going to work on you, Lynda," Pat explained. "Because that's the only person you can control."

I tried to see her point. For a whole three seconds, I gave it some serious consideration. But why couldn't this intelligent, insightful woman see that I was emotionally frickin' depleted?

I glanced at her desk and noticed Pat's happy, well-adjusted children, beaming from marquetry frames. *Easy for her to say*, I simmered. *I'd be fine*, I wanted to tell her, *if everybody else would get their act together. What did she expect me to do? Ignore the twenty-seven armed octopus that kept sliding its creepy tentacles around me, locking its little suction cups down, and pulling me under? Like daily?*

Instead, I blurted, indignantly, "Control? You think I have control? What control? I've been dealing with other people's shit for years."

And then, I launched into another rant that came from Lord-knows-where and Pat, God bless her, didn't flinch.

"You know that automatic ball machine on the tennis court?"

Pat nodded.

"That's how my life feels right now! And the balls keep firing. And I've got lobs, and drop shots coming at me, and they're smacking me in the head. And those yellow things keep coming, Pat."

I was wild-eyed.

"And *dammit*," I said, my eyes welling with tears, voice wavering, "I'm wearing flip-flops and I've got nothing but this warped Chris Evert racquet I've had since eighth grade."

I paused. Then the flood gates opened. I looked down, sobbing in front of this perfectly poised woman and stared at her slender ballet flats, catching my breath.

Pat studied me for a moment, then said softly, "Lynda, look at me."

I mopped each cheek with the back of my hand, and reluctantly met her gaze.

She placed her palm over her heart, in a gesture that signaled acceptance. Right then, I thanked God and Amelia for leading me to these still waters.

That first day, Pat took my hand and led me to the trailhead, like a seasoned guide setting out over terrain she'd covered many, many times. For now, she held the compass. I would have followed her anywhere.

In the months to come, Pat's office would become the safest place I knew.

Probably because Pat was in it.

The hour I spent with her each week became sacred. I would *move mountains*, as my grandmother Nonnie would say, cancel appointments, and ignore other crises to get to her office.

"Your children are watching how you redefine your partnership with their father," Pat reminded me, one afternoon when I was griping about my ex, rapt by the sound of my own voice. Pat never lost sight of the big picture, even when I was hell-bent on being small-minded and petty. "They're young, but they're absorbing everything. You're planting the seeds for their own relationship patterns."

"No pressure there, right?" I quipped.

"So our job," Pat continued, "is to identify your hot buttons. Once you recognize them, you can change how you react when they're pushed. You'll gain control of your responses to Stuart on a case by case basis. We're going to make conscious decisions. With each little snag, we'll determine how you can respond—gently but firmly,—to bring down the level of conflict. I'll hold your hand through each interaction, as it comes up."

"Give me an example."

"Like, when you're trading off the kids for weekends. Or you have to talk about money. We'll practice appropriate responses over and over until they become second nature."

"Lynda, every person comes into a marriage carrying the belief-system they learned from their family of origin. We don't even think about these personal truths, but they drive our decision making."

"So what's a belief system...like linen napkins on the dinner table? Or going to church on Sundays?"

"It's bigger than that, but yes. And a belief system is just the first map you've been handed." Pat explained that we are attached to the illusions we've created for ourselves and our families; how we're supposed to look to the outside world. Thank God I didn't have to face the Pinterest boards of adorable families in their clever houses back then. "Our job is to figure out what map, or belief system *you're* working from."

———

Even though she taught school all day, most nights my mother had dinner on the table at 6:30. How had she managed to run a gracious home, dote on her students and handle the tower of paperwork that came with her job? I'd patterned my marriage after hers because that was all I knew. I never stopped to define my own terms. The harder I tried to recreate the family I'd grown up in, the more glaring the differences became. Whether it's a fall football tailgate, a Labrador puppy, or a blue blazer, these outward symbols of shiny-happy-familyhood had been imprinted in my DNA.

Maybe our divorce hadn't caused Sam's problems. I looked at my friends Ruthie and Scott. Their marriage was sturdy. They communicated, didn't they? They'd formed a unilateral team. Still, their child was struggling as helplessly as mine. Could it be that this wasn't all about disjointed parenting?

I'd been carrying a long list of subconscious assumptions about myself, our parenting and Sam's addiction. Now, this layer of myths was beginning to peel away. I was a long way from a deeper understanding of secrets and shame. But I'd noticed a crack in the wall. I was one step closer to breaking through the thick veneer.

"So I'm trying to live my life from someone else's script, and it's not working? Is that what you're saying?"

Pat nodded. This was starting to make sense.

After I exposed my outdated notions about marriage, Pat encouraged me to challenge the illusions I'd attached to parenting. My own mother and father believed that a child was molded by strong values, fresh milk, good DNA, three squares a day and church on Sunday. I tried to follow in their wholesome footsteps. Still, I was powerless over Sam's path. How much control did I believe I had over him anyway?

And once the disease of addiction takes over, you can't separate your child from the side-effects. They become lazy, unreliable, and volatile. And these symptoms look an awful lot like character flaws.

———

If your self-worth is all tangled up in someone else—your child, your husband, your best friend from college—like last year's string of Christmas lights—there's a pretty good chance you're codependent. The tricky thing is that, much of the time, codependence looks an awful lot like parenting.

I had a sneaking suspicion that I was its very own poster child.

"The work in therapy is to confront your own reality with the most awareness and availability that you can muster on any given day. Some days, you'll be more clear-eyed than others. So you wake up and you drift back to sleep. And you wake up again and you yawn and stretch, but then you fall into a deeper sleep. It's a process, Lynda. Two steps forward, then take a nap. Reckoning with your own truth takes time."

"Why is that?"

She paused and looked into my eyes, sizing me up to see if I was ready for what came next.

"Because if you woke up all at once, it would kill you."

CHAPTER FOURTEEN

Running Into Myself

"Is there something you can do, just one thing, that's yours?" Pat asked as we were wrapping up another session.

"Well, when my friend Amelia's husband is out of town, I go over to her house for a glass of wine. Or, I meet my friend Annie at the back fence to sneak a cigarette."

Pat stared back at me, waiting. I knew I hadn't hit the mark, so I kept babbling.

"And, I'm on the decorations committee for the auction at Charlotte's school."

Silence.

"I bought a yoga mat?"

She was clearly unmoved.

"Lynda." I detected extreme restraint on her part. "This has got to be a priority."

I knew I was failing the test, because I couldn't fully understand the question. I left her office that week with an assignment: Find a goal that has nothing to do with my children, ex-husband or my extended family and work it into my life.

———

Thank God for my friend Camille, a mother of four with bionic energy. Camille had an uncanny ability to pinpoint where she was needed, and she'd put me on her to-do list, right alongside her design projects, fabulous dinner parties and the turbo-schedule of anyone with a couple of kids—or four.

All I had to do was follow her lead. Only I didn't know where we were going.

The week after my fortieth birthday, she wheeled into my driveway after she'd spotted me in the garden. She threw the car into park, rolled down the window and leaned out, announcing, "I know just the thing to turn you around."

"Around where?" I asked, looking up from the sweet basil I was planting. She wasn't buying my *I've-got-everything-back-under-control* facade.

"I'm signing up for the New York City Marathon. And you are, too. We'll train together. All you have to do is show up."

I would have followed Camille into a foxhole if she could help me shake the paralysis that had taken hold. Anxiety had wrapped me up in a straitjacket, and I couldn't pull free.

Hesitating, I remembered that Camille wasn't one to take no for an answer. "Oh all right," I sputtered, " I guess I'm in."

Later, it dawned on me she'd hit on the answer to Pat's assignment. This goal was separate from my children or their father, my brother, my parents or my other friends. Just me, Camille and 26.2 miles of New York City asphalt.

———

"I've got it," I said to Pat the following week, settling into my chair in her office and aligning myself with her angled footrest.

"Got what?"

"My assignment. I did a little chair-shimmy out of excitement. It's all figured out."

"I'm all ears."

"The New York City Marathon. I'm training for it."

"Wow, you don't mess around, do you?"

I felt proud as a peacock, and I owed it all to a tenacious and devoted friend.

Camille planned our training schedule, told me what time to wake up, what to eat and when to go to bed. She rang my phone at 4:45 a.m. for extra measure. She mapped our routes and pulled me through all five hundred miles of warm-up. She even designed the red t-shirts we wore in the race.

For the crack-of-dawn runs, I worked out a system with my neighbor Annie. An early riser, when Annie's girls were at their Dad's, she'd scurry through the back gate into my kitchen, bright and early, wearing pajamas, coffee in hand, to read the paper and keep an ear out for Charlotte, who wouldn't wake up for another hour or two.

With a brother carted off to a wilderness program and a father she mainly spent time with on weekends, Charlotte had more on her plate than a lot of first-graders I knew. But the tension that held us hostage had dissipated a bit and Charlotte skipped a little more lightly these days.

She threw herself into her neighborhood friends. They put on dance shows, traded Beanie Babies and spent hours bouncing on our trampoline. I was glad to see the distance she was putting between herself and the upheaval in our family.

But she hadn't been totally immune to the strain. No siree.

———

One night, a few months into our *new normal,* we were standing at the prepared foods counter in the grocery store. I looked down at her innocent little head, and a big bad situation came into focus. There, on her right temple, where her hair should have been shiny and full, I noticed a patchy, thinning area. What was going on? How had that happened?

She'd started twirling her hair, a childish habit I thought at the time, in kindergarten. I tried not to bring it to her attention. *She'll outgrow it,* I thought, *just like she'll outgrow Lucy, her floppy stuffed lamb.*

But Charlotte's absent-minded hair-twirling was leaving a permanent reminder of the pain she was determined to mask. I felt stomach acid bubble to my throat as I looked at the spot on her scalp that she'd worried nearly hairless. It came at me in full focus, high relief, like the drill-down scenes in hospital television series, when the camera goes tracking through an intestine to locate the malignant tumor. I knew without a doubt this child was silently screaming, and I hadn't been able to hear it. Until now.

I thought I was going to vomit.

"Charlotte," I said guardedly. "My tummy doesn't feel well. I have an idea. Let's take our dinner and go on home. I'll come back for the groceries tomorrow when you're at school."

Tears pooled in my lower lids as I left the half-filled cart in the store, took her hand and steered her through the check-out line to pay for our dinner. She looked over her shoulder at the cart we'd left behind, bewildered, but dutifully trotted off beside me.

Once home, we went into the kitchen, and I picked up her compact little body, plopped her on the counter and gave her a bear hug.

"Charlotte, honey? Your hair seems to be a little thin right here," taking two fingers and gently rubbing her temple. "Can you tell me about it? Is that from when you twirl your hair?"

"I play with one hair," she offered. "I try to find the perfect one."

"The perfect one?"

"The one that feels best. It's the smoothest one. I look for it 'til I find it."

"And then, what do you do?"

"Sometimes, I pull it out."

Then she paused, catching herself.

"But not every time."

She looked down at her hands which were clasped squarely in her lap.

"Okay. It's just that your hair is so beautiful, and you don't want to have hair holes like your Grandfather or that lady we sit behind in church."

I didn't press the issue. By now, I was utterly drained. We ate our dinner and readied for bed. But the next morning, I speed-dialed our favorite nurse practitioner at the pediatrician's office. Eight-thirty on the nose.

"What the hell, Marjorie?" I whispered into the phone, even though no one was at home. "Is she pulling her hair out? Is she rubbing it off like a newborn? What is going on?"

"Hmm, I think I know," she reassured me. "Get her in here tomorrow, and let me take a look. I'll have a casual conversation with her."

The next day, Marjorie prescribed a mild anti-anxiety medication.

"This is temporary. It's just enough to get in between her and this habit. Hopefully, it will break the cycle. Then she gave me a got-your-back stare over Charlotte's head and made the pinkie-thumb signal for "call me."

I was horrified.

Confused.

Charlotte was the one perfect piece of my screwed up family dynamic, and now *she* was pulling her hair out.

Literally.

How had one child's problems bled over onto another? This thing is contagious. How long had it taken me to notice?

I didn't dare mention it to Camille during our morning runs. I couldn't mention this to anyone. One was bad enough, but, somehow, the fact that both of my children were struggling with psychological setbacks was exponentially unthinkable. I felt like a failure as a mother in every sense of the word.

A six-year-old has every right to be free from worry.

Except mine wasn't.

Siblings, I would learn later, never escape the fallout of family trauma. They become caretakers, keepers of the peace, repositories of anxiety, as if absorbing and holding the pain will somehow soften the blow for everyone around them. They become used to being the family footnote. They don't require or merit hours and hours of discussion and time and energy but live in the quiet shadows of turmoil. And they never, ever want to cause trouble. There's enough of that going around to fill every-body's plate. They wouldn't dare heap on another serving.

When I got Marjorie on the phone the next afternoon, her tone was measured. This wasn't just a touch of anxiety. It had a giant, honking scientific name: *Trichotillomania.*

"What the hell is that? The word's bigger than she is."

"Hair pulling. It's an urge, triggered by anxiety or depression. Lies on the obsessive-compulsive spectrum. So the hair pulling is the symptom but it's rooted in emotional distress. We see it in this age group. Peak on-set is nine to thirteen, so she's a bit early."

When you Google it, trichotillomania falls right in between its ugly stepsisters, anorexia, bulimia, and cutting. It's all about control. I knew a girl in elementary school who didn't have any eyebrows or eyelashes. Her hairless face flashed in front of my eyes. *So that's what that was.*

"They don't even know they're doing it, usually," Marjorie contin-ued." When it happens, the child is in a trance-like state. The gratifica-tion that comes from pulling the perfect hair is about relieving tension. These kids are too young to talk about how they feel, so this becomes a self-soothing behavior. Like a pacifier. I really think the medication will help. It's a short-term solution. Our goal is to break the cycle by lowering the chemical stress response. The next best thing for you to do, though, is to talk with a child psychologist, for a future strategy."

I tried to take it all in.

"And Lynda?"

"Yes?"

"Don't put yourself in a tailspin. She can feel your stress. Just know that we're addressing it. We've got a diagnosis, that's half the battle."

At another time, I might have been inconsolable. But I hadn't reached my threshold, not just then. Besides, I didn't have that kind of time.

Training for the marathon gave me a place to blow off steam. By now, we were up to twenty miles in one day, and I could feel the therapeutic effects. I was physically getting stronger. I was mentally feeling tougher. And I believe that strength carried over in my ability to handle this latest hair crisis.

"It doesn't surprise me," Pat said when I told her about the hair pulling. She's such a self-contained little nugget, those feelings have to go somewhere. This is how it's manifesting itself. But if you're in a panic about it, she'll sniff out your fear like a bloodhound and that won't help."

I gulped.

I was terrified.

Only now, I didn't let the terror paralyze me. Instead, I picked it up and took it to the streets. As I ran, I imagined sweating that toxic terror right out onto the Richmond pavement.

———

"So how's it going?" Pat opened our next meeting, folding back the sleeves of her silk-knit tunic and adjusting a gold bracelet.

"I'm trying not to watch Charlotte too closely. I know it'll make her skittish."

"I'm not asking about Charlotte right now." Pat nodded, as if she was talking to a small child. "You know where I'm going with this."

"Oh! You mean, me?'

Pat looked patient.

"Yes, you. We're really here about you, remember? If we're doing a good job working on you, Lynda, the rest will fall into place." She spread her hands out wide, arms to either side, then shrunk them in palm to palm, leaving a little sliver of light in between. She was always calm when she said this. And she said it a lot.

As the weeks passed, I started picking out the sound of codependence—or lack of it. I was getting it. The idea wasn't quite so abstract now. I could see it in action, hear it in my voice—on the phone--or in conversations with other people, too.

"So I said to him," Camille spurted out breathy fragments one morning, tracking through the byzantine labyrinth of her schedule, "If you want to play golf once a weekend, I'd love to see you do that, but I need you to help Charlie pack for his Scout hike on Saturday. I have a last minute client meeting."

"I understand Tuesday's busy for you," I'd tell Stuart over the phone. "But that's the only day I'm free to meet." Before Pat, I would have turned myself upside-down to accommodate him, or anyone else who asked, frankly.

"Pat, it worked like a charm," I marveled.

"See what can happen when you change your response?" she lit up, excited to see me finally putting her wise words to work in my life.

I knew how each choice, each compromise, had chipped away at my own fibers, my own identity, until I hardly recognized myself anymore. I wished my mother had hammered home the fact that there's nothing selfish about honoring your own needs. You're actually strengthening your marriage.

"You do what you know," Pat explained. "It's tribal. Your mother did a lot for your father. How would you know anything different?"

She had a point.

Charlotte and I settled into a comfortable rhythm. Life was sweeter.

For the moment.

Marjorie filled me in on a secondary symptom that hair-pulling creates: shame. "They're too young to understand, but somehow, they know what they're doing isn't quite right. A lot of energy goes into hiding the behavior, which, in turn, sets up a whole other set of psychological bugaboos. But, Lynda, you got on it quickly. A lot of parents can't wrap their heads around it, so they pretend it's not happening."

Charlotte's hair was filling in, and her spirits seemed lighter. Perhaps, because she was no longer keeping her shameful secret.

———

The marathon training gave me a burst of adrenaline. Still there were mornings I'd beg off, evenings I'd screen Camille's call and training runs when it felt like I was dragging a flatbed. I wasn't perfect, but I stayed focused. And it felt good.

By September, Camille's training program ramped up to four mornings a week, with longer distance runs on Sundays. When marathon weekend finally arrived, we boarded the train like two college girls heading off on a Big Apple adventure. Our cheering section would arrive the next day, our brothers, their wives, our parents and Camille's husband, James.

Every step on the twenty-six-mile course was taken with a single-minded intention. This was my race to run. And I wasn't about to let myself down. When we entered Central Park, my brother broke from the crowd to run the last five miles with us, our personal cheerleader. As we crossed the finish line in triumph, squarely in the middle of the pack, I felt a lightness of spirit I'd lost during the dreary months I'd spent mired in the dissolution of my marriage.

When Pat had given me her assignment, *pick something that's about you and work it into your life,* I couldn't imagine shoehorning one more task onto my to-do list. Hadn't I already shoveled too much into my one-pound bag? And wouldn't a wise therapist encourage me to subtract—not add—to my burden?

But in the marathon's sweet afterglow, I understood. Pat and Camille had opened a door. Just for me. As I stepped through, I'd tapped into a strength I didn't know I possessed.

In spite of sure progress, Charlotte was still twirling her hair. Renovations on my single-mom house were taking on a life of their own. Stuart continued to dodge my bids to compare calendars, and Sam was once again serving detention that weekend at Elkin Academy, where we had paid to have his wilderness program extended into the school year. My problems hadn't really gone *anywhere*.

But I was changing. And while my problems still overwhelmed me some days, they no longer defined me. I was something more.

Guided by Pat's wisdom and Camille's tenacity, I was reframing. Nothing had changed. And yet *everything* had.

"I did it!" I told Charlotte when she answered my phone call.

"Mama got the mare-thon!" she squealed, calling out the news to Stuart.

"And how many miles in a marathon, sugar?"

"Twenty-six point two...yoooouuu!"

"And you can twenty-six-point-two, too, Charlotte. One day, you can do it, too!"

After a massage and a hot shower at the hotel, we joined our families for a victory dinner. The next morning, our support group left for the airport. Camille and I headed back to Penn Station, dog-tired, but still giddy. We found facing seats and stashed our duffle bags against the windows, melting into them like pillows, as the train clattered south toward home.

"I never in a million years thought you'd take me up on my brilliant idea," Camille mumbled from her side of the aisle.

"You didn't?" I asked. "Well, I've got a worn-out body to prove it."

"Shocked the hell out of me, that's for sure," Camille said, drowsy. "I just wanted to wake you up. You were a mess, Lynda." She waved her hand toward mine, palm flat. "Now look at your bad-self. High five, Sister."

CHAPTER FIFTEEN
The Porch Light

I'd love for Sam's problems to be my fault. Really, I would. I'd take responsibility while walking barefoot over razor blades if that would pull him back in-bounds.

I'd been seeing Pat for a year now. I couldn't shake the question of blame. What was my accountability here? What responsibility could I shed, and what did I need to own?

"Parents who think they have total control are sadly mistaken," Pat reminded me. "The superstar child that fuels their parents' self-worth? It's the flip side of your problem, only with trophies. Whether we're talking about addicts or superstars, no parent has complete power. And here's the difference, Lynda: Nobody comes to counseling to cope with their overachiever."

Pat's truth resonated. I knew the type well. They surrounded me. These onlookers took full credit for the trophies, the straight As, the merit scholarships. Their children's permanent records stood unblemished.

Maybe a tardy slip.

A library fine.

Nothing more.

And they stood back, arms folded across their smug chests, looking me up and down, buzzing amongst themselves, playing both judge and jury. Like a Greek Chorus, they chimed in with unsolicited opinions and advice.

Have you tried grounding him?

You need to set limits.

Put the rules in writing.

"One mother advised me to *just say no and mean it*," my friend Lang sighed, years later. "Trust me, I've said *no* until my throat bled. Does she think I'm a freaking idiot? He was unfazed. He's been insatiable ever since he sucked on a pacifier. His default emotional state was: *I want it now.*"

Some children are just more compliant by nature. Their parents are quick to chalk it up to their own exceptional disciplinary skills. "Right," Lang agreed, ever the cynic. "They're stellar parents until they have a difficult child. Then all hell breaks loose."

The blame is palpable. And you dutifully pick it up and drape it over your shoulders, cloaking yourself in shame. The unspoken message, of course, is this: *If you were doing your job, your child wouldn't be so screwed up.*

Anyone who's been battered and tossed on the waves of a difficult child becomes a little bit broken. I've read the parenting books. I've seen the specialists, tried the chore charts and remedial reading programs. I've chased down more answers than the Greek Chorus has questions. Unfortunately, like many in the same boat, I somehow internalized the blame; came to believe that Sam's problems all led back to me.

Maybe I wasn't doing enough. Or maybe I was doing plenty—but of all the wrong things. When alcohol and drugs arrive on the scene, the parent of an oppositional child can become beaten down by second-guessing, by hope, then failure, shame, guilt, blame, maybe wishful thinking. I'd lost my internal compass. I knew in my bones what was right. But once I started swaying to the rhythm of the family dance while tapdancing to distract the Greek Chorus, I no longer trusted my own instincts. And I couldn't fix anything, or anyone, until I fixed myself.

When Anne Lamott was writing *Wounded Birds,* her novel about Marin County teens, she asked *her* son, Sam, what he would tell a parent who was watching a child slip deeper into drug abuse.

"I'd tell them to get their own help first," he said, without hesitation. "No child is going to listen to a parent who's freaked out. You're no help to your kid until you get yourself straight."

I appreciated the friends who tried to walk beside me, really I did. Although their facile advice was well meaning, I'd started to feel divebombed by flying monkeys. I'd given too many people access to my control panel, Pat explained.

But those friends didn't sit at my breakfast table during those rollercoaster years. They hadn't attended the bleak teacher conferences that foreshadowed boarding school for a fifth-grader. Or endured the broken marriage, yet another ingredient in this toxic stew. And they hadn't dragged their seventh-grader through the grim barracks of a therapeutic wilderness school in West Virginia, and left him there, praying the $60,000 tuition would buy a miracle.

For a flicker, it did buy a miracle. And when Sam came home for spring break, making his bed unprompted and asking what he could do to help around the house, I tried not to let my excitement get out in front of me.

"Perhaps the worst is behind us?" I pleaded to Edith Goldman as Stuart and I contemplated eighth grade, Sam's next step. What a luxury it would be if the next school would see him through to graduation.

With her connections and blessings, we enrolled Sam in Rappahannock Prep, an Episcopal boarding school on the banks of the Rappahannock River, at the mouth of the Chesapeake Bay, with an excellent sailing program and an enviable academic tradition. Their admissions officers could be counted on to overlook an applicant's youthful transgression—or two. Perhaps Sam's maturity was catching up and the years we'd invested in specialized education were finally paying off. My heart beat a little faster.

"So happy for you and your family," chirped a peripheral friend at Yellow Umbrella seafood, welcoming me back into the mainstream school club.

"Rappahannock Prep!" announced another. "My nephew from Winston-Salem is there."

But my relief was short-lived. Sam was just fourteen, a few months into eighth-grade, when alcohol staggered on the scene, like an uninvited guest, stubble-faced and foulsmelling. The first time I witnessed Sam drunk, he was home for the weekend and turned up at the house on a Saturday afternoon, stumbling into tables, knocking over lamps, moaning and belligerent.

I thought he might be having a seizure and I tried to guide him to the sofa. He pushed me off with such force, I knew I was in over my head. I called Stuart for backup. In hindsight, we should have taken him to the ER to rule out alcohol poisoning. Instead, we let him sleep it off.

The next morning, remorseless and defiant, he refused to tell me what he'd been doing the day before, with whom he'd been doing it and where he'd gotten whatever it was that caused such freakish behavior. "What's the big deal?" he argued. "Everybody does it." Thank God Stuart was driving him back to school on Sunday, back to dorm counselors and curfews.

Sam would finish Rappahannock Prep under a cloud. Although I never saw him in *that state* again, I'd find beer cans and liquor bottles stashed in his room or outside under his bedroom window, after weekends at home.

Now, in addition to a hair-trigger temper and fleeting attention span, Sam was showing emerging signs of substance abuse. For some children, normal teenage experimentation flies under the radar. It's invisible, a counselor once told me. It may have no lasting effect. It usually doesn't manifest itself in suspensions or expulsions from school, repeated DUIs or overnights in the city jail. But for others, it could very well be catastrophic. These are the adventures of an addict and he's just getting warmed up. Sam's grades were dismal and when the administration at Rappahannock Prep insisted he'd violated their computer usage agreement, I suspected they'd simply had enough.

"Stupidest thing," Sam sniped. "I downloaded a picture. So what?" If I'd had evidence in his favor, I might have gone to bat for him. Instead, the school rubberstamped a passing grade on his eighth-grade transcript, allowing him to advance to ninth. Somewhere else.

Back-to-school shopping had taken on a new meaning. Each summer, we found ourselves researching a new school for the upcoming fall. Next up, an alternative Richmond school—River City Academy. For a slightly longer moment, I could exhale again.

Slowly, imperceptibly, Pat was repairing my broken infrastructure, fortifying it, beam by solid beam. She shored up crumbling walls, ripped out rotting foundations and reinforced the weak spots.

"You *know* this stuff," she reminded me. "Trust yourself. You got the framework growing up; your parents worked together; they modeled consistency. Your instincts are dead-on. But you've lost your confidence.

Was it any wonder?

And you're looking outside of yourself for answers. They're not there. You need to get back to your own truth. It's in you, I promise."

———

It was a summer Saturday. Our new house on Toddsbury Road was starting to feel like home. Sam was living full-time with Charlotte and me for the first time in well over three years. The phone rang right before dinnertime.

"I'm spending the night with Mac," he announced.

I bristled at his arrogance. Why is a fifteen-year-old telling me what's what? It doesn't work that way in my book. It never had. I'd just forgotten.

And in that moment a memory flooded back. I could hear my own mother saying, *Whoa, Nellie. Why don't you run that by me again?* I stood up straight, struck by the recollection of my father raising his palm to signal halt, in full support. *You don't tell us what you're doing,* he'd rumble. *You ask. Politely. And you wait until we give you our decision. And that's the last word, understood?*

I'd been undermined for so long that I'd forgotten the template my parents had given me long ago. My core values had been marginalized. And I'd lost my voice. But I was on my own now. And I had Pat in my corner. I'd crushed the New York Marathon— in my mind—sold a house

137

and pushed through a divorce. I was standing tall again. I could hear my parents in the background, loud and clear. A righteous, loving, indignation welled up inside of me, from right where it had been stored all along.

"Sam." I steadied myself. "Number one, you don't *tell* me what you're doing. You ask. Clear? And number two, I want to call Mac's mother to make sure it suits her."

Defiant, Sam shot back, "You're not gonna call her."

"Sam, of course I'll call her. That's just how it works, buddy." I steeled for the tirade that followed. Absent, this time, was my own fear.

Bring it on, big boy. You're not the boss of me.

Back and forth, we volleyed:

Won't.

Will.

Will.

Won't.

Finally, I hit the overhead smash.

"Sam, I don't appreciate your tone of voice. So how about we do this?" I drew in a breath, lowered my voice, and spoke slowly, deliberately. "You. *May not.* Spend the night. With Mac. And I expect you home. By 11:30." If I'd felt more confident, I would have ordered him home right then and there. But I was already sticking my neck out waaaay beyond my comfort zone. If I'd stopped to think about my answer, I might have lost my nerve. But I stood firm, propelled by a core certainty. I knew I was right on this one. And I added, "If you're not home by 11:30, the front door will be locked. Do you hear me?"

Silence.

Did I think he was going to high-tail it home at 11:15 to meet my 11:30 p.m. curfew? Hadn't he gotten exactly what he'd demanded in the first place—a night of unbridled drinking and pot-smoking? What if my strategy backfired? Hadn't I just given a fifteen-year-old a perfectly good excuse to stay out all night? Maybe so, but I'd taken a stand.

Months before, I'd confiscated Sam's house key after he broke into my rental house and threw a party. Now, I was leveraging that small advantage to build on my newfound conviction.

"Is that clear?" I continued, hoping I sounded stronger than I felt.

"Whatever."

I heard a click, then a dial tone. I stared at the phone in disbelief. *If I'd ever talked to my own parents that way, I wouldn't have lived to tell the tale.* I paced the house for the rest of the evening. Thank goodness Charlotte was spending the night at a friend's.

And thank goodness I had Robert.

———

We'd been together for over a year by then. I'd gotten into the habit of crawling under the covers at night with the telephone. And that night, anxious for comfort, I dialed his number.

"If he doesn't come home, stick to your guns," he said, ever reassuring. "Trust your instincts. I know Pat would support you in this, and I do, too. I'll check on you in the morning." It felt good to have an ally. Robert was teaching me to trust myself again.

Distracted by a hot shower, at 11:30 on the nose, I locked the doors, turned out the porch light, climbed the stairs, and went to bed. The digital clock screamed 11:40 and I lay awake for God-knows-how-long, cussing, crying, praying and seething at Sam's defiance. I wanted more than anything to hear a knock at the door, to run downstairs and let him in.

Was he smoking pot with a friend whose parents were out of town? Was he walking angrily down the side of some highway, fair game for any predator? And how would I explain to others that I locked my fifteen-year-old out of the house? At night? How would I bear the recrimination if things went horribly wrong? If he got hurt, how would I live with myself? I was desperate to know he was safe. And I hoped Sam had a conscience that might be bothering him right about then.

Years later, I would replay this decision with a Richmond residential rehab counselor with years of experience working with addicted teens and their parents from every socio-economic rung on the ladder. She listened with a wry smile: "A parent's definition of what's 'safe' is upside down and backwards. 'Safe' is when a kid knows their parents aren't going to tolerate abusive behavior. And if that means locking a door to hammer home the message, so be it. There are limits. Parents freak out but, these kids? They know exactly where to go when they're locked out of the house. Are you kidding? They won't end up on a park bench. I tell parents, they'll be fine. You're just withdrawing the perks: the cozy bed, the maid service, the well-stocked refrigerator." She spoke from personal experience. Her own mother kicked her out of the house once during her rebellious teenage years. "Best decision she ever made."

Still, I worried about our children in cars. About drug-fueled binges. And I couldn't bear the possibility of my own child hurting someone else's. And wasn't I also worried about the Greek Chorus? What if Mac's mother found out that my son slept at her house because I locked him out of mine? What kind of mother would that make me?

But it wasn't about me anymore.

I wished the parents who sat in judgement would spend an evening wrestling with these questions. Tough love sounds simple in theory. On paper. But when you're applying it to a very real child—one you want to strangle fairly frequently, one who can be volatile and menacing, a child you love with all your heart—it's another thing entirely. It's a lot like landscape design. Plotted on graph paper, the foundation plantings might look brilliant, but the grand design doesn't always take root in the field.

I thanked Robert for listening, praying he hadn't noted the suitcase full of rocks I was dragging into our relationship. I stared at the ceiling, trying to keep my anxiety from creeping up the walls like black mold. Eventually, I drifted into a restless sleep and woke to the first hint of morning light streaming through the woven blinds. As I padded sleepily downstairs to retrieve the newspaper off the front steps, I half-expected to find Sam curled up on our Pawley's Island porch swing. When he wasn't there, I felt oddly relieved. For at least a few more hours, the house would be peaceful.

Late morning, Sam called, starting in on me again, every bit as arrogant as he'd been the afternoon before: "I can't believe you fucking locked me out, Mom."

"What time did you *try* to come home, sweetie?," keeping my voice steady.

"Doesn't matter."

I gathered my authority, shaky as it was. "I did exactly what I said I was going to do, Sam. What part of *that* can you *not* believe? And do not speak to me in that tone of voice. Do not use that language with me. I've always been willing to compromise, but it's clear you want to run the show. That does not work for me, Sam. And if it doesn't work for you, call your father."

"Whatever," he said again, dismissively.

In that moment, something inside of me snapped. Why had I been crawling on all fours around this kid? I let him have it with both barrels.

"On second thought, Sam, you have until this afternoon to get your clothes. Tell your father you'll be staying with him for a while." This was a whole new experience for me. Just then, I didn't need to lobby for support from anyone else. I operated from my core, and it was liberating.

In standing up to Sam, I would be creating some much needed structure in Charlotte's life. My convictions would make her feel safe, protected by firm rules instead of the shifting sands of inconsistency. Charlotte needed to see the structure in our household. Pat had made that clear.

She *deserved* a home that was safe from constant chaos.

She *had the right* to a mother who could occasionally focus on *her* needs.

She had the right to go to sleep at night knowing that I wouldn't be rushing to a police station with bail at two a.m.

She had the right to a mother who could sit down to dinner without being on high alert.

She had the right to make her own mistakes, to fall down and know that an emotionally available parent would help her get up.

She even had the right, when the time came, to rebel. A little. The quiet, well-behaved adolescent who's afraid to rock the boat is almost as worrisome as the wild-child. She may be sitting politely with hands folded neatly in her lap; but she's also suppressing the necessary boundary-testing behavior that transitions a child out of adolescence and into adulthood.

Ask any sibling of a difficult child, especially when substance abuse is concerned, and they'll tell you they wouldn't dare get into trouble. One Book Club sibling sobbed to her stunned mother: "You have no idea how hard it is to be good. I work hard to *not* get in trouble; to *not* act like my friends. You know why, Mom?" she said, through tears of frustration, "Do you? I do it because you and Dad cannot handle *one more thing."*

These siblings know their parents have reached their limit. They can't cope with more beer cans, cigarettes, bongs, and broken curfews.

I recalled the balding spot on Charlotte's head, reminded of Sophie's choice: *If I can save only one child, which one will it be?*

I was learning to stand my ground. Find my voice. With Pat's guidance, I was considering my own convictions and actively defending them. Of course, parenting as a unit is the goal, but we don't always get what we want. On the upside of an acrimonious divorce, you no longer bend to accommodate a spouse who rarely had your back in the first place.

Had Stuart and I been under the same roof, I wouldn't have had the option of kicking my son out of the house. Had we still been married, I might have caved because I couldn't picture a refuge. *Where would he go? And to whom?*

That day, I figured Sam and I would take a little break. Blow off some steam. A week, maybe two. Then pick up again.

But we don't always get to choose the outcome either.

Sam would never live with Charlotte and me again.

CHAPTER SIXTEEN

Team Triage

My parents had a solid, old-fashioned marriage. Like every couple since Adam and Eve they didn't always agree but they didn't need a library of parenting books to operate as a team. When a decision was required, they'd disappear into our knotty-pine paneled den and close the door while my brother and I waited on pins and needles.

When their muffled squabbling ended, they would emerge together—my mother straightening the bobby pins in her hair, my father's face flushed from hushed arguing, —and present a united, if disheveled, front as they announced the verdict.

Most times, we could have guessed the outcome. My parents rooted their principles in traditional family values and good common sense. And, if nothing else, their decisions were predictably and annoyingly consistent.

"No," they'd declare, "you may not invite your boyfriend to the beach for our family vacation."

"Yes, you'll be attending your second-cousin's wedding, even if it means missing the homecoming dance."

"No, you may not have a car for your sixteenth birthday. We don't care if Mary Margaret Gillespie got one."

My brother and I didn't dare question their decisions, not in front of them, anyway. In our house, their word was law.

I figured all marriages worked that way. And so I'd felt a twinge of alarm, even in the early days, when mine didn't.

During our carefree dating years, Stuart was charming and spontaneous. We spent beach weekends with friends, shot skeet at his parents' farm, and once he presented me with a dozen French tulips "because it is Tuesday."

Once we were engaged, we needed to make joint decisions.

"Sure, babe. We'll talk later, okay?" he'd say, heading to the tennis court.

"Whatever you think. Fine by me."

And when I got a job offer from a law firm, he was all smiles: "They're lucky to have you. Don't think for a minute they don't know that."

The teamwork part would come later, I rationalized. And wasn't it nice that he trusted me to pick out the china pattern and decorate the nest? Even after we married, we were still thinking like two single people. Our biggest decision each day was dinner. "How about that chicken thing you made last time?" How could I complain? He was so agreeable.

This worked for a while. Until it didn't.

Once children entered the picture, I realized something felt amiss. Their very lives depended on us working as a team.

But where were the thoughtful discussions?

The weighing of pros and cons?

The joint decisions?

Did we want a fixed or adjustable-rate mortgage?

What was our policy on bottle versus breastfeeding?

What did we want in a preschool?

Would we kneel with our children to say bedtime prayers?

And if so, which ones?

By the time Charlotte came along, I couldn't ignore the fact that Stuart and I were operating from wildly different playbooks.

Had the tension in our marriage reached a rolling boil just because of Sam's issues?

Or was it all of the above?

Even healthy marriages can be torn apart when school problems and substance abuse enter the picture. Like the black light a crime scene investigator waves over the hotel bedspread to expose forensic evidence, these parenting stressors can reveal the ugly parts of a marriage.

When Stuart came home the night of my Roslyn Road meltdown, it didn't occur to me to share the depth of my despair with him. I'd withdrawn more than I realized. We'd cultivated neither a shared set of principles, nor a sense of teamwork. No wonder I wasn't feeling heard or validated. He probably wasn't either.

When the children were little, most of the discipline fell to me and, I'll admit, I liked it that way. But as the need for teamwork and household structure increased, the great divide became more and more apparent. And as the need for cohesive parenting increased, so did my anxiety.

Once Sam's issues entered the picture, the marriage lacked the infrastructure that might have sustained us. Could we dress up and hit a charity ball looking like we dovetailed perfectly? Of course. But when problem-solving skills were needed, our marital toolbox was just plain empty. We'd tied a knot in the rope and clung to its frayed ends, muscles trembling with the effort, but we couldn't hold on any longer. We were both exhausted.

For years, I blamed our divorce on Sam's problems. And later, at a rehab family weekend, Sam blamed his problems on our divorce. Still, I've talked to enough addiction experts to know it's not that cut and dried.

"Marital status has little bearing on how well two parents support a child in recovery," says interventionist Bill Maher, a national expert in the field, whom we would meet years later. Having worked with thousands of families during his career, Maher observed, "I've seen divorced parents work brilliantly as a team and married couples, who can't even admit the child is headed for trouble, undermine each other at every turn."

What does a young person in the grip of addiction need from his or her parents? Maher says it's one simple thing: a heart connection. "Parents need to be working from the same book, the same page, the same paragraph. If I don't see that heart connection in the first visit, I may tell them I can't take their case."

Teamwork means thinking ahead to set policy. Find a counselor to walk you through tough decisions. Then ask yourselves, how will we respond to an arrest? Bail him out in the middle of the night? Or let him stew in jail for a day or two? Make these decisions together, when you're not under duress. Know in advance when you'll shut off their phone, confiscate car keys, cut off the money. Then do it. Follow through. Hope for the best, but plan for the worst. You'll be a far more effective parenting team.

At-risk children can drive a wedge between their parents with the precision of a martial artist. Like lab rats, they've figured out which buttons to push. They align themselves with the parent who lends the money, hires the lawyer, bails them out, gives them another chance—or fifty.

That parent, the enabler, cushions them from the consequences of their actions. The enabler is often too busy, distracted, or exhausted to take a harder line. So they sweep their child's escalating substance abuse under the rug, ignoring it as long as they possibly can.

With a child's first crisis, marriages that are already showing loose threads may quickly unravel. Other couples pull away from family and friends out of shame or fear of being judged. They lose their support system when they need it most.

When I published these thoughts online recently, in a blog post titled *The Wedge*, my cousin emailed me the next day: "Lynda, *seriously?*"

"Seriously, what?" We'd talked recently about her daughter's drug use and she and her husband were at odds about next steps. "I thought our conversation was confidential," she snapped.

I wasn't thinking about her marriage when I wrote that post but clearly, it struck a raw nerve. I would never blithely violate a friend's confidence. But she was certain it was her marriage I was writing about, her trust I'd betrayed. "This *wedge* I was writing about?" I ventured. "It comes with the territory." I wanted to say, "*Trust me, you didn't invent it. It's* not a specific event with a beginning, middle, and end. It's a chronic condition, sharper some times than others."

Married or not, the challenge lies in how a couple faces tough decisions.

Sam possessed a particular genius for getting between Stuart and me when a big decision was on the table. "Why spend all that money on a wilderness program when I don't belong there?" he'd press, after he'd burned every bridge in a string of boarding schools. "The kids there are freaks." If that didn't work, he'd turn menacing: "If you send me, I'll run away. You'll be sorry." More than once, he threatened to kill himself in protest. Invariably one of us would cave to this song and dance, leaving the other one feeling undermined.

Seven years later, a letter from Sam confirms what I'd always suspected. These kids know what they're doing. And they don't take much pleasure in it, either.

"Dear Robert," he wrote to his step-father, *"I've started this letter over now for about the fifth time. I'm writing you because I feel that I owe you a huge apology for all the strain I've put on your marriage. Please do not take it personally because I've been on a course of self-destruction well before you and Mom were together. I want you to know that I do care a lot about you…I just feel like the biggest disappointment of all time when it comes to my family.…Please take care of Mom and yourself. Much Love, S."*

Granted, the skills required to parent a high-intensity child don't come naturally to most of us. We need to stuff our pride in our pockets and ask for help. Too often, a child suffers while the parents shoot in the dark.

The best advice I ever got: whether your marriage is made of stone or it's crumbled beyond recognition, focus on clearing a single channel of communication where the child is the priority. Everything else between you—the grudges, tensions, petty squabbles, skin-crawling irritations— are off-limits.

We've brought these children into the world. For better or for worse. And we don't have the right to act like children ourselves. They need us. And we're bound by a shared obligation to work together on their behalf—-always in triage mode.

CHAPTER SEVENTEEN
White Picket Fence Divorce

Over the next three years, I observed Stuart and Sam living more like roommates than father and son. At first, I'd imagined dinners with Sam and Charlotte on Tuesdays and Thursdays, the orderly arrangement I noted on television shows or among my few amicably divorced friends. Sam and Charlotte would maintain ties to both parents and to each other. I'd traded my white-picket-fence dreams of marriage for the fantasy of a gracious divorce. If my family couldn't remain intact, I was determined to create the most congenial, well-adjusted, broken family that ever didn't live together.

But the joke was on me. And Stuart wasn't reading that same fairy tale. His idea of co-parenting was to tell me what he'd decided, after the fact. "This doesn't concern you, Lynda," he spat back when I emailed a list of my suspicions. "He's living with me. You're not paying his bills. I'm in charge here," closing his reply email with, "Bring Charlotte over Thursday night. We're going out to dinner."

With Sam under his roof, Stuart pulled the plug on me, like an outdated lamp headed for the dump. Even Sam treated me like an unwelcome intrusion. Unclipped from the decision making loop, I lost day to day contact.

If Sam had a curfew, he routinely ignored it. This news filtered to me through friends, whose own boys envied his free-range lifestyle. But Sam was out of control, even loose acquaintances hinted too loudly for me to ignore.

And I'm convinced he progressed from drug user to drug dealer during those high school years. One friend-of-a-friend, a woman I'd met once at the garden center, pulled me aside in the vegetable aisle to mention that she'd seen Sam's truck cruising her neighborhood at lunchtime on a weekday. "That's odd, don't you think?" she said, surveying the fresh brussel sprouts.

"I'll look into it." I assured her, feeling grateful, with a side-dish of irritation masking my shame.

Two months later, when Sam was arrested on drug possession charges, the legal merry-go-round was set in motion. His license would be suspended; then he'd be stopped for speeding, found in possession and charged with driving on—you guessed it— a suspended license.

Stuart was unmoved. "It's just a phase," he said, dismissively. "Boys. They get in a little trouble, but it all straightens out in the end."

Without his father and me on the same page, one doctor after another had echoed Edward Brooks' frustration. "I can prescribe medication all day long," the last doctor sighed, "but it's worthless unless this young man has the scaffolding in place to support him." With no psychiatrist, no medication, no therapist or tutor or rules in place, Sam was left to chart his own self-destructive course. And he was getting in trouble as quickly as Stuart could bail him out.

Through it all, Pat never wavered.

"Hang tight," she'd counsel. "You have clearly been given the back-off notice, Lynda. The most important thing you can do now is to create a healthy structure and a safe place at home for Charlotte. Remember, when you commit to being a stronger parent to her, that's when Sam will take you seriously. He'll know you mean business."

"So I'm not supposed to fight for my child?" I countered her, frantic. "I just give up and play the victim?" I'd never talked back to Pat, but this came close.

"It might look like you're giving up on Sam," Pat said. "And it's tempting to jump into the ring with all of this testosterone. But as you step back and stop reacting, you'll see the power in remaining on the sideline. It takes more than one person to create conflict. Don't be a part of it. It might look like apathy or abdication of power, but it's the opposite. It's a source of connection, strength and clarity. When you're in the eye of the storm and you're chasing Sam, cleaning up his messes every time he gets in trouble—and you're begging Stuart to communicate—you get sucked into the chaos. Stepping back is counterintuitive, I get it. You're uncomfortable with that. But you'll see. Eventually it works."

———

Without Pat, I would have become a marionette. Jerked awake by the middle-of-the-night phone call from jail, hurrying downtown to find Sam there, unrepentant. Arranging for his release. Paying off fines and lawyer fees. And the message I'd be sending? *Go ahead, sweetie, break the law. I'll save you from those big bad cops. And I'll run myself ragged to do it.*

"Children are raised within a circle of accountability," says Barbara

Burke of the Family Counseling Center for Recovery (FCCR) in Richmond. "Picture a ring of concentric circles, like dropping a pebble in a lake. The first circle is the family. That's the bull's eye. For most kids, family rules provide healthy boundaries. But if the child can't operate within those rules, then the school takes over. That's the next ring. They're suspended or expelled. And if school sanctions don't deter them, there's the local law enforcement. And the next ring is the state police. Then they advance to the federal system. It's up to that child to decide where it ends."

"What does Stuart think? I was just an incubator?" I demanded, during one rainy day session with Pat. Sam was limping through his junior year of high school, at a local day-school that had accepted him under assurance from Edith Goldman.

Two years earlier, I'd visited River City Academy with Sam for an admissions interview and had been put off by a student body punctuated with ear gauges, body piercings, chain wallets and an array of hair colors, none found in nature. Call me shallow, but I couldn't picture my Sam fitting into this mix.

"How was the visit?" Dr. Goldman asked the next day.

"Um …. I liked the school—it's the students I'm a little worried about. The girl who showed us around had a tongue stud and was a little on the Goth side. I'm not sure Sam would find any friends there."

"Oh?"

I was walking into my own trap, but I couldn't stop.

"What makes you say that?"

"The kids looked like freaks." There, I said it.

By now, I'm tripping all over myself.

"Mrs. Harrison, Sam has far more in common with those students than your blue blazer boys down the street." And she nodded her head in the direction of St. Boy's. You may not like what they're wearing and I understand it's hard for parents when a school or its student body doesn't match their picture; but trust me, those young people are trying to overcome various and significant obstacles—just like Sam. River City Academy is tailored for young girls and boys who happen to be dealing with a lot of his same challenges. And by the way, they've graduated some pretty impressive students."

———

By now, Sam's behavior ran so far afoul of my own values that my skin crawled. How could I convince my close friends that I fully disapproved of my child's behavior? Did they know I was helpless to change it? How could I reconcile it myself? I wasn't brought up that way. It's not the way I'd ever raise my child, given the choice. He was flagrantly defying every rule of civilization as I'd known it—driving without a driver's license, hosting parties at Stuart's house, running that small business from his car— and I was mortified.

With each new disaster, I felt my own reputation take a hit. No sooner had I righted myself and redeemed the last scraps of my dignity, Sam would turn everything upside down again. One Christmas Eve, we were sitting in a pew at church, Sam looking like a million bucks, in his navy blazer and jeweled tie. I beamed with pride, but as I watched him drift off and jerk awake with a start, my pride turned to horror. Sam was floating in a Percocet haze right there as the choir above sang like angels. I had conveniently overlooked the sling holding his arm—a friend had broken it with a baseball bat, settling a drug dispute. Even a near-perfect moment like this wasn't safe from the chaos in Sam's life.

"I'm going to say this to you until I'm blue in the face." Pat held firm. "I'm going to remind you at every session. Sam's behavior *does not* define you. It is not who *you* are. And the work we have to do, and it may take time, is getting you to see that you're a separate entity. We need to get you to a place of awakening and self-awareness, beyond what other people think of your parenting. The goal is to ingrain in you a sense of competence that's independent of your child's success or failure."

"Even the grandfathers have met to discuss this nightmare," I told Pat. "This is so foreign to my father's experience, a child who lives with just one parent? And has no accountability to the other? In his mind, it's wrong on so many levels."

"Any progress there? How'd that go?"

"The two of them sat in a coffee shop; my Dad made no bones about the fact that Stuart was discounting my role as Sam's mother. That when one parent undermines the other one, it's practically criminal. My Dad said he'd support our family any way he could but, at the end of the day, Stuart and I needed to parent this teenager from a unified front. Stuart's father was in total agreement.

"They talked for two hours."

"And?"

"Nothing's changed."

———

I'd learned to take nothing for granted but, by April of his senior year at River City Academy, Sam was on track to graduate. It had taken four schools and a year in the wilderness to get there. I was cautiously overjoyed. On the big weekend, his stepfather flew in from Pennsylvania. His aunt drove over from Roanoke. Both sets of grandparents were there, mine traveling up I-85 from South Carolina. And when they called his name, sweet Charlotte gave my hand a squeeze.

But Sam's father didn't see him walk across the stage to receive his diploma. Graduation had fallen on the same weekend as Stuart's annual fly-fishing trip. Stuart spent Sam's graduation weekend at the mountain resort where our marriage had ended five years before. "Sam told me to go ahead," he explained later. "He said it was fine." By now, Stuart had invested hundreds of thousands of dollars in tuition and therapy for Sam. I decided to focus on that fact and chose gratitude over anger.

Still, I was crushed for Sam. In my white-picket-fence dreams, his father was right there to celebrate the greatest achievement thus far, in his short, turbulent life. Instead, he'd given his Dad the easy out and an easy answer, even if it wasn't all true. Their relationship is their relationship. I'm sure they would celebrate in their own way.

His diploma in hand, Sam was grinning from ear to ear. And behind that smile, I sensed a small flicker in him that said, *maybe I can do this.* I allowed myself the momentary luxury of thinking it, too. *Maybe he can do this.*

He knew exactly where he wanted to go next. And I rather liked his plan. He would move to Colorado and attend a two-year program at a community college. He was reaching for the mountains, the fresh air, the music scene. The academic pace would support him. He'd make a clean start.

Maybe, just maybe, we were seeing the light. Maybe Sam would hit his stride. And maybe we'd look back with a sigh of relief someday. *Phew! What a rough patch it had been,* we'd all agree. *And aren't we lucky we've pushed through it?*

CHAPTER EIGHTEEN
Wassup, Girl?

everal of us in Book Club were managing blended families while the others' marriages were first-and-only's. Those vintage relationships may not have been quite as scintillating and spontaneous, but through thick and thinnest, they were still standing strong. And that was no small accomplishment.

The "Newlyweds'" bedroom topics elicited ear-covering mock horror from the oldschool wives. "It's called *land-scape-ing*." Lang enunciated, as if addressing a trio of elderly foreigners. "Nobody goes native anymore. You should try it," she added, elbowing Ruthie. "Go get yourself a Brazilian. You'll feel like you've lost five pounds, and David will think he's having an affair right in his own bed."

"Too much information!" Ruthie cringed. The rest of us laughed at her, relieved for the subject-change away from parole officers and drug tests. Book Club conversations ranged from sex toys to salad dressing recipes, from heroin to housekeeping. From lost marriages to the prospect of losing a child.

Ruthie had no idea that a "rabbit" was also a vibrator until we showed her a picture online. We're still not sure if she knows what to do with one. That Christmas, when we exchanged presents, Ruthie unwrapped her box, finding a bunny ornament tucked inside along with a gift card to Kiss & Make Up, a local adult novelty shop. Our tag read: A reminder of the possibilities! Love, The Newlyweds.

Ruthie groaned and shook her finger at us, then made a big show of tucking the gift card into her bra. You won't find that kind of exchange at Al-Anon.

It was my turn to host. Always the first to show, Ruthie sauntered in with an exaggerated, "*Whassup Gurrrrl?* Dinner smells good." She picked up a baby carrot and dragged it through the bowl of hummus I'd set on the counter. "God I've missed seeing you," she said as she grabbed the hem of her windbreaker and pulled it over her head. I looked up from the cheese-wafer dough I'd been slicing and waggled my knife. "Don't get too close. Sam's at it again, and I'm about ready to use this thing." She pulled up a counter stool and sat down, her mood shifting. "What happened?"

I dropped the sliced rounds on the cookie sheet, pressing each one a little too hard, like it was to blame. "Robert and I checked the court docket online, and there's no way on God's green earth that child can possibly have a job. 'Mom,' he says, when I have him on the phone and ask what's going on. 'I've got it under control. It's not your problem.' And I hear him pull on a Marlboro, slowly exhaling. He's trying to play me like a fiddle."

"I get that from Liz. Makes you want to wring their little necks, doesn't it?" She leaned forward and scanned the counter, her eyes landing on the cookie sheet. "What's that you're making?"

"They're from Alabama. Mamie's. Real-deal homemade cheese wafers. Libbie Market freezer section. I keep a roll on hand for emergencies, and right now, my whole life feels like an emergency."

"Like slice-and-bake? I could probably handle that." Ruthie chuckled as I slid the tray in the oven. I turned to face her, arms pointed heavenward, with the oven mitt still on my hand. "If he's so busy getting arrested and going to court, how in the hell is he financing his cross-country band tour following Widespread Panic and String Cheese?"

As a mother, you learn to read the blank pages. A job they don't mention is a job they don't have.

"I wasn't born yesterday. As my father says, I didn't just fall off the turnip truck."

Just then, headlights glanced off the windowpanes.

"Here comes Lang up the driveway. I think Celeste rode with her. Sally's running late. She had a parents' meeting after school. This'll keep. You sure as hell don't want to hear it twice."

Lang walked in looking like a million bucks, as usual.

"Okay *where'd* you get that jacket?" I blurted.

"That place on Cary Street," she said, looking proud of herself. "Sale!" She walked straight to my open laptop on the counter and ran a riff on the keyboard. "Here, lemme show you. It comes in three colors."

"Lang would look good in a burlap sack," Celeste said from the front hall, shutting the door behind her with her foot. "But, you're right. It's damn good looking."

Ruthie peered at the screen over her shoulder. "Oh Lord." She waved her hand and made a face like she smelled something rancid. "How do ya'll wear that stuff? I'd look like I was playing dress-up."

"Well, it won't work with Danskos, that's for sure." Lang quipped.

"Don't mess with my Danskos," Ruthie shot back.

159

"How hungry are you guys?" I said, motioning for them to pipe down.

"Did you fire up the grill? I'm starving," Lang said, looking over the laptop at me. I'd picked up blackened chicken from the grill next to my pharmacy, warmed it on a griddle, and placed it on a bed of arugula. I drizzled my default dressing on top. It's a recipe I pulled from a magazine and mixed to taste: lemon, parmesan, garlic, oil, a few other odds and ends. I'm a big believer in the artful shortcut—what my grandmother would call instant replay. Book Club wouldn't have cared if I had baked a frozen pizza or picked up chips and French onion dip at the 7-11. Our sacred pact was built on honesty and support, not on fancy food and high fashion.

"Serve yourselves and sit down. Sally'll be here in a minute." I said, handing Ruthie a plate.

When she arrived, we stopped eating long enough to let her say grace. A nurse at a Catholic school, she could gather our feelings and offer them up in a prayer the likes of which the Pope himself would envy, often weaving in a news item for good measure. With Sally's blessings, our meetings felt sanctified.

"Heavenly Father," she began as she hopped up and down, shaking her arm out of the sleeve of her jacket. "Thank you for giving us a voice and friends to listen. A place to lay down our burdens. A place free from judgment. A place of peace. Bless our President and our brave troops in the Middle East. Bless the tornado victims in Oklahoma and have mercy on that poor woman who left her children in the car to get to her interview at Taco Bell. Because we're all doing the best we can, even when it isn't pretty. And protect our children. Lord knows we've tried. Bless this food to our use and us to thy loving service. Amen."

Ruthie held up her hands like a traffic cop. "All right, y'all. We have a situation here." She nodded in my direction. "You ready?" I nodded a yes, and she continued. Sometimes it helps to have an introduction. "Looks like Sam's living the high life with no job to back it up."

"Define high life," Lang said.

"He's traveling all over creation. He loses his driver's license as often as I misplace my reading glasses. There's no way he's got a job. He's too busy getting arrested. According to the Denver court docket, he's missed three court dates and racked up big-time fines from his failure to appear. I mean how is this kid paying rent? Buying gas? Groceries? Stuart hasn't answered my emails, so I'm wondering, is he financing this whole fiasco?"

"Sounds like he's dealing and someone's bankrolling him on top of that." Sally proposed.

Two years ago, she watched a drug deal go down at the end of her cul de sac. Her son, George, was either buying or selling. Who knows which. He's been in and out of jail since. He'd be released on probation, then fail his court-mandated drug test. Over and over. Sally told him she and his dad wouldn't post bail anymore.

I recalled our trip to South Carolina when I barely knew Sally. She'd hinted at problems with George, but drug use never came up. Since then, I'd seen her hang tough, come hell *and* high water.

"It's easier to stroke a check than to work out a strategy," Lang said. "If only it worked that way."

Ruthie jumped in. "Lynda, if Stuart won't listen to you, does he have a brother? Or a friend who'll talk some sense into him? If he doesn't cut Sam off financially, things are gonna get ugly."

Celeste had been quiet until now, but she seized the moment. With twelve years of sobriety under her belt, we respected her insight. "Look guys, this is what it means to be powerless. Step One, remember?" The room fell silent. "Lynda, if there was really something you could do, I know you'd do it. Right now, you can't control Stuart, and you sure as hell can't control Sam. Sam needs to accept his consequences and, Lynda, honey? You need to accept them as well."

"Here's what you can do," she continued. "You'll pay for a recovery program, but you will not post bail. You can write him a letter and remind him that dealing is a felony. Tell him you won't support *that* behavior, but you will support treatment. Anytime he's ready, you're a hundred percent behind him. He's all the way out in Colorado and you won't have every mother around here picking you apart for making him stand on his own two feet."

That's what Pat had told me. It felt good to hear it reconfirmed.

"I know it runs against everything you'd do as his mother. But the parents who bail their children out with high-priced lawyers are just asking for trouble down the road," Lang chimed in. " My ex and I don't exactly see eye-to-eye, but we've worked out a deal on the money piece. I text Greg to give him a head's up if I pay for something for Caroline. That way, we both know how much money that child's drawing from *The Bank of Mom and Dad.* We've caught her double-dipping for textbooks before, asking us both to pay. You've got to close that gap."

"There's an old joke in AA," Celeste added, "How do you tell when an addict is lying?"

"I don't know, Celeste. How do you tell?"

"His lips are moving."

That one got a good laugh from the dinner crowd.

Ruthie grabbed the oven mitt and waved it around. "Gotta share this one, guys. I ran into a friend whose daughter has an eating disorder. It's the same as addiction in a lot of ways. Her child's in the grip of another ugly disease. So, you know what she did? She named that nasty old eating disorder 'Fred'. That way she separates the disease from her daughter. And when her child's in the grip of her disorder, my friend pins it on 'Fred'. 'Fred's at it again,'" she says.

Compassion welled up for my boy, my Sam. He had a whole lot of "Fred" in him these days. All of our children did.

We continued around the table, sharing news, trading updates. I was at peace with these women who'd been wrung out in the same spin cycle as me. We steadied each other. We stacked the plates, loaded the dishwasher and said our goodnights.

One day at a time.

We'd made it through one more.

CHAPTER NINETEEN
The Red Door

More disturbing news trickled in from Colorado. First, Sam got a traffic ticket. Then a hit-and-run charge. And by the time he was booked on possession, Sam's illicit behavior had swallowed massive chunks of his life and eroded the friendships that had steadied him so far. The string of recent downturns had cost him his apartment. He'd slept in his car until it was impounded after the hit-and-run. Then he couch-surfed, relying on one friend, then another, until he wore out his welcome and moved on.

Without a mailing address, Sam's life became a tsunami of missed court dates, unpaid bills, unattended probation visits—a legal quagmire that eventually crashed and flooded into a wreckage he never even connected to his drug use. Pat says we often have to reach a crisis point in order to initiate change. "An episode. Something harrowing but, God forbid, not fatal," she'd explained. But Sam's denial ran deep. It was clear "Fred" was running the show. I began another urgent search for help.

———

I'd heard the stories of Book Club children hitting a wall that forced them to confront their self-destruction. Celeste's son didn't remember the rain delay that sent him and three baseball teammates home to down a couple of beers. He couldn't recall returning drunk and belligerent to the diamond once the skies cleared. Or how he'd kicked and flailed as three fathers wrestled him to the asphalt and into her husband's car for the trip home. He'd skinned his knees and elbows and woke up the next morning wondering what had happened. "I saw dried blood everywhere," Charlie said, "but, I didn't remember how it got there. And it freaked me out. That was it. I knew where this was headed."

I was envious that Sally's son, George, had awakened his parents for his late night confession. I prayed for "a knock at my own bedroom door," followed by Sam's heartfelt plea. If not, he'd wind up back in jail or dead. I was sure of it. At twenty-two, he was incapable of holding onto a job, and after six weeks in jail, he still hadn't gotten the message.

Years later, I wrote a blog post that creates a vivid picture of what denial looks like to me:

> *You're awakened one night from a deep sleep.*
> *You detect the faint odor of smoke, but you hope it was just a dream.*
> *You're too groggy to get up and check the source of the smell.*
> *You roll over and attempt to go back to sleep.*
> *Eventually you do.*
> *Some time later, your senses are roused, haunted by a re-*

minder of that familiar vapor.

You sniff the air, wondering if it's in the room, here and now.

Maybe not though.

Surely, you're imagining it.

You pray you're imagining it.

But you anticipate real danger.

Wait — Now, not only can you smell something, you see it creeping around the corner — swirls of smoke and an orange flash.

Is this a vision conjured by an active imagination? A day-dream? A nightmare?

You don't want to be an alarmist.

You decide to wait and see because you're still a little sleepy.

Things could change.

The flash could die down.

Suddenly, you're fully awake. You know the truth. It's as-phyxiating.

Your house is engulfed in flames.

I'd talked myself blue in the face. I begged him to devote thirty to ninety days to his health, to stop the insanity. It was my responsibility, or so I thought, to make sure Sam's volatility didn't jump the tracks and destroy someone else in the process. What if he sold the fatal overdose? Or killed a young family in a head-on collision? And at the moment, these scenarios weren't so farfetched. But what exactly was I supposed to do?

I'd read about family and friends gathering to intervene. They'd ask an addict to 'wake up,' to break down the stone wall of denial behind which he'd barricaded himself. Pat taught me how denial fuels addiction from both sides of the aisle, with the addict and his family lulled by its warm embrace. Breaking out of denial is not a one-time event, she explained. The addict—or the parent(s)—might awaken to the severity of the situation, then drift back into denial before waking up again. It's a cyclical process.

The theory behind an intervention is that if Sam is surrounded by people who love him and hears their heartfelt testimonials about the suffering he's caused them and himself, he might see the light and agree to enter treatment. We'd already tried to talk to Sam as a family. Now, we needed a professional.

"Do you know an interventionist?" I asked a few confidants. It was like asking for a reputable witch doctor or a reliable exorcist, but I didn't care. One name came up repeatedly: Bill Maher. Not to be confused with the television pundit, this Bill Maher lived in Richmond, but like the television pundit, his reputation extended nationwide. I forwarded his bio to Stuart, hoping he'd get on board. I had no idea whether Maher would take us on, but like everybody who picks up the phone and dials his number, I was desperate.

Intervention can be an expensive, risky business. By the time you fly in a grandparent or two and pay the interventionist's fee, the tab can exceed $10,000. There are no money-back guarantees, no "Intervention Insurance" policies. The best-case scenario is that the addict slows his downward spiral. When the intervention is successful, parents earn the privilege of pouring tens of thousands of dollars into a residential treatment program and can only hope and pray their child stays put once they get there. A treatment facility is not prison. The addict-cum-patient isn't on lockdown. They can walk out at any moment. And many do.

Just short of a miracle, and to my serious relief, Stuart emailed to report that he'd spoken to Maher himself. And when I downloaded the attachment detailing Maher's process, I felt grateful that the ex-husband with whom I'd been so bitterly at-odds was joining me at the professional table. Whether he knew it or not, Stuart was taking a step that would force him to pry open Pandora's box and remain accountable for the goblins that flew out of it. I had to give him credit for that. Still, we had our work cut out for us.

Strolling past the historic row houses in Richmond's Fan district, I would never have guessed that the cheerful red door facing the sidewalk was the one we wanted. But there it was marked with a sign: William Maher." A former addict himself, he makes no bones about his rock-bottom days in the urban underbelly. He'd lived under a bridge and smuggled heroin for a drug cartel.

A clear-eyed, confident man who infused the room with the fervent energy of an evangelical preacher, Maher had nineteen years of sobriety under his belt. He'd facilitated over two thousand interventions. He listed two presidents and scores of A-list celebrities among the clients who willingly gave up their rights to anonymity. Maher could tell stories that People magazine editors would pay big bucks for. But he won't. He'd answered a calling, to calm the maelstrom just long enough for an addict to accept help.

"You've got a young man who's on a crash course," Maher began at our first meeting, after sharing vigorous handshakes all around and settling into his well-worn upholstered chair, which had heard it's share of heartache. "He's a brilliant manipulator—all addicts are—so even if you despise each other," and here he paused and looked from me to Stuart and back, "you've got to lock arms and hold firm against the manipulation.

His disease will kill him, if you—his touchstones—can't cooperate to end this madness. Right now, you're complicit in his self-destruction. You're cushioning him. If you don't stop working against each other, you're going to be working together—to plan his funeral."

Maher had spoken.

"Do you want this for your child? Are you committed to work together, despite your differences?"

Silence.

I stared straight ahead. I felt like I was accepting Maher as my Lord and Savior. If he'd asked me to shave my head and shake a tambourine, I'd have done it. I was ready to join the cult of Anybody-with-a-Game-Plan. Perhaps Maher could cut through the noxious thicket of anger and resentment that had coiled up around Stuart and me. The thorny, ragged weed had choked us to near death, and here was the machete-wielding man skillful enough to hack through the mess.

You'd think parents would set aside their differences when a child is in danger. And if Sam had been diagnosed with leukemia, somehow we would have. No question. But addiction's tendrils curl through a family like kudzu, weaving a chokehold through the generations. The lying, manipulation, exhaustion, shame, and futility of dealing with an addict sets off a chain reaction. Even the teetotalers sip this toxic cocktail, blaming, denying and feeding on resentment. The disease infects parents, grandparents, aunts, uncles and especially siblings who, Maher said, can become lifelong rescuers. The question isn't whether siblings are affected, it is how much and how deeply.

My hands folded in a prayer-like gesture in response to Maher's request for solidarity. My lip quivered uncontrollably, and tears trailed down my cheeks. I wanted so desperately to bury the hatchet, wipe the slate clean, but an anguished rage had settled deep within my cells and held my generosity of spirit in check. If we had faced Sam's reality sooner, maybe we wouldn't be hemorrhaging, emotionally and financially.

As part of the intervention, Maher asked us to make a list of people from every aspect of Sam's life: friends, family, girlfriends, mentors, coaches or counselors, all who'd meant something to him. Next, we needed a compadre of Sam's who'd already found his way out of the darkness, someone his age, and from his world.

"We are masters at compartmentalizing our lives," Maher said. "By bringing together family, classmates, employers, coaches, ministers, and friends, the addict finds people from each of these compartments assembled in one place. Probably for the first time ever, his skeletons start falling from all of the closets with stunning similarity. The group shares experiences, some sweet, some sad, some just ugly, others horrific, even despicable, and the truth—the very truth—the addict's been hiding—comes out in a safe, supportive space."

I don't think Maher was expecting fourteen people, but he didn't blink when we presented our list the following week. His fee was already in the thousands of dollars, and in Sam's case, he said we'd need backup. At three hundred dollars an hour, a former Drug Enforcement Agent would serve as Sam's security escort. Maher recommended Caron, a treatment facility located in Pennsylvania. He called ahead to secure a bed while Stuart filled out the necessary intake forms.

Home from Colorado, regrouping for a few weeks from some usual setbacks, I fixated on how Stuart and I could work together to get Sam to Maher's office at the appointed date and time. It felt like planning a surprise party. Sam was elusive, skulking around the shadowy fringes of our world. If I invited him to lunch, he'd smell a rat. Plus, I couldn't trust him to show up. Instead, we cooked up a story about Stuart getting him in to see a lawyer. With new charges pending, this got Sam's attention. We recruited his friend Michael to go along for moral support.

Team-Sam would assemble in two weeks. In the meantime, Maher would ask key people to write letters in testament of their love and concern for him. "The only feelings you can claim are your own," Maher explained. "This letter can't include speculation about his feelings, no finger pointing or blame toward Sam or anyone else, for that matter. Stick to 'I' statements. And remember, 'You' is not a feeling; so don't say 'I feel you are blankety-blank.' Avoid generalizations like always or never." *Whew.*

Ten days until showtime and my stomach rumbled like Mount St. Helens. I had no reason to believe that Sam would hear our pleas much less accept help. We'd placed an expensive bet. But we'd taken action. That much was comforting.

In the interventions we see on reality TV, the unsuspecting target stumbles into a room full of family and friends. Or is pulled from a warm bed in the middle of the night. Professionals call this the *Snatch-and-Grab* method and, in extreme cases, it's still warranted. But Maher pioneered a gentler approach. "We call it an *Invitational* or *Systemic Intervention*. We send the message that his loved ones will support his recovery but not his disease. We are committed to keeping trust intact," he explains, "which improves the chance of long-term recovery."

When you give an addict grocery money or pay his rent, it might feel like support, but you're actually funding their disease. You can love a person literally, to death, Maher told us solemnly. If you dismantle this kind of enabling, you can slow the momentum of the disease. But everyone in the addict's world has to know the game plan. Everybody has to buy in. And you all have to hold firm.

———

On the designated day, we met at Maher's office, where he'd added a dozen folding chairs to the room. I was overwhelmed to see Sam's godfather, his grandfather, aunt, several of our close friends who'd known him since birth, and his third-grade teacher, who'd buoyed us through St. Boy's. They'd all gathered in the name of love for Sam. Eight years later, my memory of the loving concern on the faces in that room can still make me weep. They'll never know how much it meant to our family.

Maher welcomed them, politely. But when he addressed the group, he unleashed the full force of his calling. "If we want to save this young man, you all need to be reading from the same book, on the same page, same paragraph, same sentence." He paused to let his words take effect, as if he was presiding over a gospel revival.

He clasped his hands, palm over palm, in a signal of unity, and his voice softened to a whisper. "This family is in pain," he said, gesturing to me and then to Stuart. "And your willingness to be present for them is an immeasurable gift. Showing up. That's what life is all about. Sam may be angry when he sees you. He may be confused. He might show relief or he may be belligerent. But whatever he does, don't, for one minute, think that deep down inside, he doesn't appreciate the fact that you're here."

We waited nervously for sounds at the door. Anticipation coated every square inch of the room, heavy with stagnant air.

What would happen when Sam walked in?

None of us knew.

CHAPTER TWENTY

No Casseroles

I was folding laundry, when my "playgroup" friend Cameron called. "He crossed three lanes and hit one of those massive, green highway signs," she reported. "Killed on impact. They think it was acid."

I'd known this boy since he turned up at our house for a playdate wearing yellow rain boots and a Batman cape. A classmate of Sam's, he was six then. Today, he'd be twenty-four. His funeral was scheduled for Thursday morning at eleven.

———

There's bad news and then there's searing tragedy. News of a child's sudden death sucks the air out of your lungs. The world stops for a split second. In that instant, one family's story is forever rewritten.

I slammed the phone down, sat at the kitchen counter and wept. For that boy. For his parents. For his brother and sisters. And his young friends. I could see his Batman cape trailing as he followed Sam and our dog, Bo, out the playroom door and into our backyard. He'd grown into a handsome young man. Another promising life lost.

In our pocket of the city, a death in a family sets women in motion. We rush to the house carrying card files and casseroles. Neighbors and friends mobilize, coaxing the grieving parents to turn their household over to us. They have no choice, really. They're meeting with the minister, the funeral home, arranging flights back east for children away at college, choosing hymns, writing the obituary. How do you sum up a life that ends before it's begun?

Their house becomes a buzzing hive of helpers and callers, door-bells and delivery trucks. We set up a card table, a hasty command center. From there, we record visitors' names on yellow legal pads, in pencil. We look up their addresses, note their offerings. When there's downtime, we neatly and efficiently transfer this information to a card file. This record of bitter loss shored up by steadfast compassion will be used for thank-you notes.

And later, years later, each index card stands as a testament to the deep reservoir of grace that ripples under our lives, even when we cannot see it. A computer spreadsheet cannot match the metal flip-top file box, which remains with the family, sometimes for generations. A tangible symbol reinforcing the message: *You are not alone in your sorrow.*

The cards. The cupcakes. The cheese straws. The contributions.

We answer the phone, and we place the orders and we clean out the refrigerator to make room for the coconut cake Eugenia Williamson lov-ingly baked and brought over the instant she heard. During the service, we designate door-answerers to stay at the house and accept deliveries. A newspaper funeral notice is an open invitation. Nobody home between three and five p.m., it announces. Someone always stays behind to protect the place.

Afterwards, young people stream through the house. They're wearing their Sunday best mixed with disbelief and confusion. So far, their experience with death has been limited to goldfish and grandparents. It wouldn't be long, I feared, before they were old hands at this.

All the while, we're secretly thanking God it's not our child, not our house, not our spare freezer filling with casseroles. But it could have been. Because we're all skating on the same thin ice.

———

By the time the Book Club met the following week, Celeste, Ruthie, and I were wrung out. We'd been with the family for days. Cece had just moved into a downtown warehouse apartment but already, an urban-hip vibe filled the space. I was a little bit jealous; to be fifty and free of a house and a yard? Everything about it felt liberating.

"I don't know how Kathryn's still standing," Ruthie said. "With the streams of people and a knife through her heart, she had to find a navy blazer and shoes for that youngest one to wear to the funeral? Did you see how tall he's getting?"

"How about a screaming yellow sweater? That's what I wore to my brother's funeral," Cece broke in. She's been our go-to source for siblings and grief. Suicide is not knowing, she reminds us. It took her twenty years to figure that out, so she shares her hard-won wisdom freely.

"I was fourteen, and no one was paying attention to me or my wardrobe. I had no idea what people wore to funerals. Yellow sweater? Check. You just muddle through, and a lot of times you get it wrong. You can't think straight when you're grieving that kind of loss. In the end, I guess wearing a screaming yellow sweater to your brother's funeral won't stop the world on its axis."

"And the food?" Ruthie broke in. "We had to send half of it to three neighbors to store in their freezers."

"Oh God, that reminds me of my friend Jenna," Cece interrupted. "Listen to this one," waving wildly to get our attention. "Her brother was killed instantly in a car accident. The other driver crossed the median. So tragic. And two days later, Jenna's mother is buried in casseroles, right? So she picks up the phone and dials. "*Hello, Sears?*" Jenna pricks her ears up from another room, but can't stop her in time. "*My son just died and I need a deep-freeze delivered. Today!*"

"Casseroles?" Lang said. "Where were the casseroles when Kathryn's child was alive? They'd be there for an appendectomy or a broken leg, right? But when your child's an addict, nobody brings you a casserole."

"What else is new, Lang? The deep-freeze story is, actually, just a wee bit funny. There's always a little humor tucked under the tragedy," Sally says. "Like my grandmother. We're gathered around her hospital bed as she's dying. And she opens one eye and says—I kid you not, '*A watched pot never boils.*'

———

Cece produced two bottles of Merlot and filled our glasses. "Celeste is out of town, right?" she said, looking furtively around the room. On Book Club nights, we stick to iced tea out of respect for her recovery. But when Celeste can't come, we drink—just a little bit—of wine.

We settled into Cece's living room. Sally fidgeted with her reading glasses. "Was anyone else hurt in the accident?" She started, then stopped herself. "I mean... What would you do if?" She waved her hands, shooing away the thought. "I can't say it. Never mind."

"What are you thinking, Sally?" I edged her on. She squirmed. She opened her mouth to speak, then stopped and wrung her hands. "It's unspeakable."

"Spit it out." I knew exactly what she was thinking. I've thought the same thing myself.

Sally's eyes locked on mine. "Honestly? It's tragic to lose a child. But you know what I think might be worse?"

"Worse than losing a child?" Ruthie jumped in.

Sally pulled her hair into a ponytail, plucked an elastic band from her wrist and twisted it up, collecting herself. "There is worse, I think..." she began. "Can you imagine if your child killed someone else? Someone's child, someone's mother?" She looked around the room. "I mean, which would you choose? Your child hits a tree and dies in the accident? Or your child hits someone else's car, kills them and survives?"

Her eyes grew wide. How had those words, too terrible to imagine, escaped her lips? "Is that bad? Is it wrong of me? Honestly, I can't think of anything worse than hurting someone else. The responsibility of another person's death? I'd never get over it."

I slapped my hands on both thighs, leaning forward. I'd been crystal clear on this particular Sophie's Choice but I'd never had to say it. Or anyone to say it to. "There's no question in my mind what I'd choose."

"You've actually thought about this?" Ruthie asked, looking like she'd been gutted.

"Absolutely. If he's drunk or doing drugs? And he's driving? I'd rather my child be the one who gets killed. How do you ever get over causing someone else's death? If that makes me a horrible mother, then I'll wear the scarlet letter."

My conviction welled up from somewhere deep inside. My certainty shocked me. I love Sam but I cannot take responsibility for his choices. I knew that for sure now. I'd found solid ground. A place to plant my flag-pole in the shifting sand. Even if it means losing him, Sam's addiction and the fallout from it need to land squarely at his feet—not the other guy on the highway, not me, not anyone else.

And suddenly everyone was talking. The dam had burst.

"I thought it was just me."

"I was ashamed to feel that way."

"Who could I tell? I've carried it inside for years."

We gave these thoughts a name: Horrible Mother Questions (HMQs for short). And over dinner that night, they started coming, fast and loose.

"Is it wrong?" Lang asked, "to secretly wish your child wouldn't come home for Thanksgiving? Because you know another holiday will just go up in flames? Or, if you're relieved that she's in jail? Sometimes I sleep better knowing she's under lock and key," Lang continued with a hint of sarcasm.

"Therapeutic boarding school gave me a peace I hadn't felt since Sam was in pre-school. Does that make me a horrible mother? I was at the end of my rope. And what about the dealers?" The room went quiet. "Because a dealer's mother carries another HMQ. I can't shake the guilt that tugs at the edge of my consciousness. What if my child is the dealer who sold the lethal dose? What if the molly, the oxycontin, the quaalude tips the scales from a trip to the ER, straight to the morgue? If my child sold that fatal hit, did he cause that death, I mean, indirectly? And, if so, does that make me an accomplice?"

My life had been derailed by one drug-related crisis after another. When I wasn't grieving the son who was riding the crazy train, I was just plain pissed. Pissed at him. Pissed at the disease. Pissed at how it had steam-rolled all of our lives. Over and over again.

Pat told me to be pissed, if I needed to. To sit with the Horrible Mother Questions. Wallow in the pain, if that's what it takes. "Give yourself over to it," she said. "This pain is real but don't let it get the upper hand," she reminded me.

Since that Book Club night, seven young people who had come in and out of our houses over the years have died. Two car accidents. One suicide. Three overdoses by a lethal cocktail.

And just like that, it clicked. I remembered that first meeting, the night we struggled with the knife-edged paradox of loving a child while letting go. We're powerless over addiction, the first step read. And we read it over and over and over. I'd had to pry my fingers, one by one, off that control button. And somewhere along the line, on my Book Club nights, among women who are just as powerless as I am, I'd gotten it.

Finally. In surrendering. In giving up my power, I'd found my strength.

CHAPTER TWENTY-ONE
Showtime

Waiting was torture.

The fourteen of us sat sequestered in awkward silence. We'd braided our lives together christening babies, toasting marriages, mourning parents and sharing countless birthday dinners over the years. Now, a question mark hung in the air. How do we *do* an intervention?

"One for the books," my mother might have commented, if she'd been among us. But I hadn't invited her or my dad. The trip from South Carolina to Virginia was too far, I'd told Maher. But the truth was more complicated. I still hauled an eighteen wheeler loaded with shame about Sam's addiction and couldn't bear to expose my parents to his gritty reality. They'd run an orderly household and raised two moderately well-behaved children. I felt deeply ashamed that I couldn't do the same. I'd encouraged Charlotte to stay put, too. Her first college semester had just begun and she didn't want to start off by missing classes.

"I still feel like I should be there, but promise you'll call me, Mom," she'd said, after conceding I had a point about the classes.

———

In the hall, we heard muffled voices. The office door creaked open. I looked away, guilty for duping my own child. We'd brought Sam there to save his life, I reminded myself, even if we'd stretched the truth to do it.

In a split-second, Sam scanned the room, sized up the situation and let out a knowing sigh. Was he relieved to get support from people who were willing to help him wrestle the insatiable beast that had hijacked his young life? Perhaps he was ready to surrender.

Sam's hooded sweatshirt and baggy khakis hadn't seen the inside of a washer in a month. His handsome face was covered with stubble, his dark hair matted. He looked like a man headed in one direction: downhill. He acted foggy, like he was coming off a drug binge and reached into his pocket for his cell phone, maybe trying to summon a getaway car to whisk him out of there.

He could have flipped us off and walked out the door. But the respect we'd instilled in him still resonated, drawing him up short. Sam knew he couldn't bolt, not with his paternal grandfather in the room. He loved him too much for that. At the very least, he'd give us the courtesy of a listen.

Maher motioned to the empty chair at the head of the circle. "We're glad you're here, Sam," he began. "A lot of people have come today to surround you with their love and support. They don't want to lose you. You all go back a long way. And we're asking that you open your mind and your heart and listen to what we have to say. That's all anybody's asking today, Sam. How does that sound?"

Sam nodded. "Um, whatever." He sank into the chair and lowered his head into his hands, studying his shoelaces.

Anyone who loves an addict has heard the old saw, "He has to hit rock bottom before he'll accept help." But Maher rejects that overly simplistic view. "Rock bottom means death for a lot of addicts. You don't let someone you love drive their car over a cliff before intervening." He didn't believe in ultimatums either. "You don't wash your hands of an addict if they don't seek treatment," he noted. "You can take a hard stance without drawing a hard line. Don't ever turn your back. You'll always love that person, but you don't have to love their disease."

Take that, Fred. Bastard.

David Sheff was probably talking about Fred in his book, *A Beautiful Boy*: "Some of the time when Nic wasn't alright, I wanted to delete, expunge every trace so I wouldn't have to worry about him anymore. I wouldn't have to be disappointed by him and hurt by him and I wouldn't have to blame myself." I had felt every one of those emotions, myself, over the years.

Maher nodded to Stuart to start. He opened his jacket and pulled a folded paper from the inside pocket.

"Son, I'm worried about you ..."

GodBlessIt, I fumed, why did it make me so crazy when Stuart called him *Son*? It sounded impersonal in an Eisenhower-era way. Did he address Charlotte as *Daughter*? Did I call him, *Flipping Ex-Husband*? Who the heck was *Son*? His name is Sam, I wanted to hiss. Instead, I tried to focus on his testimonial. *Blah, blah, blah, blah,* and I caught the final line:... "so we want you to accept help."

I was next. I packed up my sarcasm and focused on opening my heart and mind. I unfolded the letter I'd carefully tucked into my coat pocket. Palms sweaty and hands shaking, I fumbled with my reading glasses, managing to balance them on the bridge of my nose.

"Love surrounds you here today, Sam." I began. I read from the paper in my lap because my hands were shaking too badly to hold it still. "However, I am terrified about your future. Your true gifts are deeply buried by your daily struggles. I am angry and disgusted when drugs control your life. I'm afraid you'll end up back in jail, or worse, I'm afraid we'll all be mourning the loss of another promising young man. For your father, your sister and me, that would be unbearable.

"This disease has made me physically ill. Literally. Lately, I've had to distance myself from you—my own son—in order to protect my health. And because of this disease, we've missed out on building the relationship I want to have with you.

"Life can offer you amazing opportunities, but you have to be clear-eyed and present to recognize them. My prayer is that you'll be willing to spend time working on yourself in treatment so that you can return to a healthy place, both inside and out. Introspection is challenging and painful for all of us, but doing this work can bring gifts you never imagined."

Sam was a dog-whisperer. He was a talented rifleman, too. He could shoot an acorn out of a tree at five hundred yards. I could picture him training dogs, instructing trap and skeet or guiding hunting expeditions. Maybe a desk job wasn't in the cards, but surely one of these gifts could lead to something. There must be some calling he could find—something beyond this.

Sam hung his head, not making eye contact. If he'd looked up, I'm not sure I could have handled it. Was he moved beyond words, or had he shut down emotionally, just hoping to end this ordeal? Either way, my part was done, and I let out a shallow breath, afraid of breaking the spell that had fallen over the room.

Over the next hour, we heard from his grandfather, his aunt Martha and his friend Michael. When the testimonials were finished, Maher let silence hang over the room like a summer heat wave. The ball was in Sam's court.

Nothing.

"Sam, what are your thoughts about what you've heard today?"

Silence.

"Can you see how much support is right here in this room?"

Sam shifted uncomfortably in his seat, lifted his head as if to speak, then lowered it again, wordless.

"Are you open to hearing more?"

Crickets.

I was grateful when our friend, Ted broke in. "Sam, Lanier and I have known you longer than you've known yourself. And we're scared. I know there's more for you than this—if you can only reach out for help. Hear us. We're here for the Sam we know and love. The daredevil Sam who raced the go-kart down the gravel road at Froggy Bottom. The Sam who caught the biggest fish in the mouth of the Mississippi. The Sam who has a future. We know he's in there somewhere."

"Dude," Michael added, picking up on Ted's message. "We've been through a lot together, you and me." Michael was Sam's age and had struggled along the way, too. They understood each other. "Dude, this shit isn't cool. We've already lost some friends. I don't want you to be next."

I felt a shift, as anticipation turned to authentic love and concern. We were no longer Maher's dutiful backup players. Our friends threw their hearts into the ring, chiming in to reinforce the message. They retraced Sam's past. They chuckled at his humor, his talent for mischief, and his uncanny ability to wriggle out of tight spots.

Finally, his grandfather spoke, his voice cracking with a plaintive tone I'd never heard before. "I love you, buddy," he began. "And all I can do is get behind you. I want us to go back to the mountains and shoot skeet. I want to run the dogs and go fishing with you. You've always been my sidekick, and I miss our time together."

Sam stared intently at the floor, unable to respond.

Maher broke in: "There's a car outside waiting for you, Sam. And we're asking you to accept this help. You can't beat this demon alone. We're all in agreement that inpatient treatment is the healthiest decision you can make right now. You'll have thirty to ninety days to focus on yourself. We've found a program in Pennsylvania. They're ready for you there. You don't have to go alone, Sam. Dave here, will make sure you get there safely." He pointed to the DEA agent, who'd appeared at the door, on cue. "He'll help you settle in."

Every year, families across the country compromise their financial security by taking out second mortgages on their homes, borrowing from family members and retirement funds to send an addicted loved one to wilderness programs, therapeutic boarding schools, and from marginal to high-priced rehab facilities. The cost of an inpatient program ranges from twenty to fifty thousand dollars for thirty days. Most often, this first inpatient treatment will not be their last.

Sam sat chewing the cuff of his sweatshirt and picking at his shoelaces, clearly uncomfortable. But he was still there. He hadn't walked. I waited to see what would happen next.

"What do you say, Sam?" Maher pressed, ever so gently.

Sam shoved his hands in his pockets. Still focused on his shoes, he said: "I don't know what you're thinking but I'm not going anywhere for thirty days. I mean, I'll like…I'll try it for two weeks. But I'm not making any promises."

More silence.

Maher was experienced enough to wait it out. He needed more than a halfhearted concession. And he wouldn't be the first to blink.

Nobody dared draw a breath.

We waited.

Then abruptly, Sam's mood shifted. He stood from his chair like he'd forgotten a critical business meeting. "Nope, never mind," he said, still looking at the carpet and shaking his head in disgust. "I don't have time for this bullshit. I'm outta here."

He made a move towards the door, and the DEA agent, all two-hundred-twentyfive pounds of him, coolly, unhurriedly, stepped into his path. "Let's you and me walk outside together and talk," he said softly, meeting Sam's distracted gaze and gently guiding him toward the door. Maher followed them, raising his right palm toward the middle of the room, signaling us to remain still.

He needn't have bothered. Left alone, we slumped in collective exhaustion and looked warily at each other. Not a word was spoken. Had the outpouring of compassion gotten us nowhere? Hard to imagine. Outside, we heard something about keys. They'd taken his car keys.

"Shit, man," Sam growled over Maher's muffled voice. He wouldn't be driving anywhere today.

We waited. My handsome, charismatic, maddening baby boy was teetering between life and the Devil-only-knows. And whatever happened out there on the sidewalk would determine whether the Devil had won.

Fifteen excruciating minutes later, the door opened, and Maher stepped back in. Expectantly, we searched his face for clues.

"He's on his way," he said, finally.

A wave of relief tinged with regret overpowered me. *He'd left already? I wouldn't get to say goodbye?*

"He didn't go quietly, but he's going. And that's what counts. Dave will get him there. He's done this many, many times, and, rest assured, he can handle anything Sam throws at him," Maher added.

I looked around the room at the shell-shocked faces. We thanked them all, as they began to stand, gathering coats and briefcases and pocketbooks, ready to return to their lives. Ted would go back to his office downtown, Lanier was scheduled to meet with a client, Michael had to be back at the restaurant to work the dinner shift. Maher had a consultation on his calendar, and I wanted to get home to call Charlotte. Sam's grandfather was the only one who remained seated, looking like a deer in headlights.

As people came to shake our hands and hug goodbye, Stuart and I stood side-by-side, as if we'd just hosted a lovely party.

"Keep us posted, Lynda," Stuart's sister said, reaching out and rubbing my arm. When you have his address, send it to me. I'll write to him." And she would, for sure.

We'd come together.

We'd dug deep.

We'd laid our beating hearts,

our guts,

on the table.

All for Sam.

And now, *could he meet us halfway? For his own sake?*

CHAPTER TWENTY-TWO
Back Porch Graduation

W e were sitting cross-legged around Celeste's coffee table, dip-
ping chopsticks into a platter of sushi, when Cece took up the
oven mitt. The conversation had turned to disappointments, the dashed
dreams we never dared mention. "You preach, you teach, you reinforce,"
she said. "But you're talking to a wall, mostly. Then one day, the clouds
part, the sun peeks through, and they surprise you. The message sinks in.
Your effort gets rewarded. That's a parenting paycheck."

In Book Club, parenting paychecks are scarce as hen's teeth. Addiction holds hostage the milestones of youth. Visions of graduations, summer internships, mission trips and college roommates stand before you
in *Technicolor*®, sadly out of reach.

"Nate's high school graduation?" Cece began. "We held the ceremo-
ny on our back porch with six dining-room chairs lined up in two rows.
Yep. Crepe paper streamers in school colors and, for music, *Pomp and
Circumstance* downloaded from iTunes. His dad picked up a *Certificate
of Achievement* from the office supply aisle at Rite-Aid, a last-minute diploma. Nice touch, I have to admit."

Cece's son, Nate, had been kicked out of the same boarding school twice. The first time, he'd been caught smoking pot. Six months later, the school readmitted him. Then, just days before final exams, senior year, he and two friends bought a "suitcase" of beer—that's a thirty pack. When Nate staggered back to the dorm, clumsy and belligerent, the dorm mom was still awake and waiting. The school called at one a.m: *Come get him.* Cece and her husband drove two hours in the middle of the night, praying they'd get home before daylight so their tenth-grade daughter, Ella, wouldn't wake up to an empty house.

"They FedEx'ed his exams, so he earned his diploma. But he wouldn't walk with his class. No cap and gown. That graduation fantasy? The one you wait eighteen years to witness? Nope, we didn't have that. It sounds selfish but, yeah, we felt cheated. I never admitted it, of course."

Cece assumed Nate had learned his lesson with the first expulsion. But his substance abuse just went underground. He drank beer behind a backyard shed. He swiped a bottle of bourbon from his grandfather's liquor cabinet and turned up glassy-eyed at Easter dinner. One morning, a neighbor called at nine a.m. "I found him passed out in a pile of leaves, back in the alley," he told Cece. The neighbor's son had died from an overdose and the concern in his voice was heartbreaking. When Nate wandered downstairs for breakfast, mid-morning, she noticed a single dead leaf clinging to the back of his sweater. If it wasn't for the neighbor, that leaf's significance might never have surfaced.

"Where do you send an eighteen year old?" Cece questioned. "Betty Ford?" My brother snarled, "He needs to be at Hazelden." His own children were in middle school, but suddenly, he's the authority. I felt two inches tall. Judged. But a counselor said, *Save your bullets. He'll rebel against a 90-day program.*" Still, you can't just stand there wringing your hands."

Help came one night when Cece's friend, Louise, dropped off her daughter for dinner with Ella. An Episcopal minister, Louise had just officiated a wedding. She joined Cece at the kitchen counter, wearing her clerical collar and sipping a glass of wine. When Nate staggered in the door, obviously drunk, Cece was horrified.

"Have I taken you on a tour?" she asked Louise, abruptly looking for a foil. "Come see the finished basement!" Downstairs, she whispered through gritted teeth, "What the hell am I supposed to do? Call the cops on him?" Louise scribbled a number on scratch paper. "There's a place in town. Call them. Ask for Barbara."

A substance abuse counselor and a revelation, Barbara gave Nate a risk-assessment test. "Nate?" she explained. "Some people can't handle caffeine. Some can't do sugar. And some people, Nate? They physically cannot process alcohol. It's not a moral failing or a lack of willpower; it's just your chemistry. Everybody's different."

"No judgement," Lang interjected, "that's a novel idea. So how'd the test go?"

"Surprise, surprise. The next week he was found highly likely to abuse alcohol. He walked out of that appointment knowing how he'd need to manage himself going forward. But the real saving grace was this: When Nate messed up senior year? I knew exactly who to call. We hauled his ass into an outpatient program the next week. And he's defiant, right? He doesn't think he belongs there. And you know what that counselor said to him? She said, 'Nate, you may not have a problem with alcohol, but alcohol has sure caused some problems for you.' We were ready," Cece said. "And that made all the difference."

"Good point," Celeste added, "Whether he's just a party boy or a bona fide alcoholic, if it walks like a duck and quacks like a duck, the consequences are the same."

"Wow that's a pretty great number to have in your address book," Suzanne said, laughing.

———

"What's so funny?" Lang sounded irritated. Sally was losing it and Cece was falling apart, too. "I'm sorry but I'm remembering a dinner," Sally shot a look at Cece, who was now doubled over. "All the pretty young things. This young mother had moved to town from Atlanta and my friend, Adele, hosted an address book party for her."

"Address book party? Is that something they do in Atlanta?" I asked, poking at the wasabi blob in my soy sauce.

"So everybody brings phone numbers to share with the newcomer. You know their favorite upholsterers? Caterers? Interior designers? People brought contact info for faux painters, that great alterations lady, oh! and that farmer who brings the pony for the birthday parties, right?"

"That's a sweet idea," Ruthie said. "I remember that life. Back when I thought those were the only numbers I'd ever need."

"Am I right?" Sally said, looking to us for the buy-in. "So Cece and I start writing down everybody we've got on speed dial. You know, the child psychiatrist, the criminal defense attorney, the marriage counselor, the divorce lawyer…"

Cece cuts in "…forensic accountant, bail bondsmen, tow-truck driver and…" Now she's laughing so hard she's snorting. "… a pet crematorium. But we cut that last one and just stuck with the happy-family stuff."

"Bet ya'll were a big hit. The wet-blanket sisters?" Celeste shot back as she brought a platter of brownies in from the kitchen.

"Jeez, I'd have killed for that list, I cut in. Seriously, what a timesaver."

Cece may have been blindsided when Nate didn't graduate with his class, but back then, every time I dialed an expert's number, I received more damning evidence that Sam was offtrack. In our culture, we've tacitly agreed on a timeline for a young life: kindergarten at five or six, college at eighteen, marriage by the late twenties. But for Book Club mothers, all timing bets are off.

"Comparison," Pat counsels, "is the riptide that will knock you to your knees. It's not always the reality that pulls you under," she says. "It's the expectation that goes unfulfilled. We're attached to the illusions we've created for our families." Cultural conditioning, she calls it. "We grow up believing life should look a certain way. So if generations of your family graduated from college, and your child drops out, that's your unfulfilled expectation. And it's crushing. On the flipside, if you grow up on the mean streets, you're lucky to make it past twenty-one without getting shot, or arrested, or overdosing. Totally different set of expectations there. It's a miracle just to survive."

I spent years trying to keep Sam on track. When he wasn't progressing in lockstep with his peers, I wondered if other parents noticed. I worked hard to keep up appearances. "Look! Fifth grade, right after fourth! Imagine that." But after a while, my arms got tired of holding up the whopping illusion. I'd been seized by the creepy-crawly sensation that something awful was coming. I just didn't know what. The burden had grown heavier and heavier. Finally, I let the illusion crash to the ground. The blood rushed back into my arms and it felt so good to stand solidly in my own truth.

"You've got to challenge those illusions. Identify the expectations you've held in a white-knuckled grip. You can't control the outcome," Pat said, gently. "Just stay present. Find grace in something good. Don't let comparison become the lens through which you view your world." Still, I held out hope that someday I would have some proud news to share. At that, Pat would nod serenely, reassuring. "Remain open to that possibility."

"Brownie?" Celeste offered.

The back porch graduation represented letting go of an illusion. I'd stared down my own illusion years before. The connection struck me, clear as day. I took a brownie and grabbed the oven mitt.

"Hey ya'll. I've got a question. How much energy do we put into trying to *look* normal?"

"Well, if it was a paying job, I'd be living on a yacht in the French Riviera," Ruthie joked.

I waved everybody in with both hands, "Guess what happens when we make an honest effort to just...be honest?"

"What are we being honest about now?" Celeste called from back in the kitchen.

"Our friends take on the job, because they want us to look normal, too. It's like everybody's invested in maintaining the social order, keeping things in balance."

"Like, how?" Ruthie added, contemplating her brownie.

"Okay, I bought the cutest, fattest, most fragrant tabletop tree for Christmas one year. And you know what happened?"

"What?" All three said in unison as Celeste took her seat.

"All hell broke loose, that's what."

A live, ceiling-scraping tree is the centerpiece of the Christmas illusion among my friends. After my divorce, and after putting up and taking down countless oversized Douglas firs, usually by myself, I challenged that holiday illusion and called bullshit.

"How about we do a tabletop tree this year?" I asked Charlotte, when she was in middle school. "It would be just as pretty, only easier, right?" Charlotte took it under advisement. But once she mentioned this proposition to her friend, Lizzy, my phone started ringing.

"Lynda, have you thought this through? Lizzy's mother, my friend Lanier inquired, panic in her voice. "A tabletop tree? Seriously? Is that really fair to this child? After all she's been through?"

"It's not pink aluminum, for crying out loud," I stammered. "It's a live tree that'll drop needles all over my floor, just like yours. Only smaller." Still, she'd ignited a flicker of doubt in this Christmas mother.

At my next appointment, I mentioned to Pat how *Treegate* was exploding around me. Pat puzzled my account for a moment, then spoke slowly: "So a tabletop tree means you love your children less, is that it?" It looked like she was trying to keep a straight face. "And Lizzy's big tall tree means her mom loves her more? That's the illusion, Lynda. Don't you see it?"

I did, I guess. I just needed to shore up my convictions. Pat's office was the perfect place for that. When you free yourself from the burden of maintaining illusions, it's liberating, like riding a bicycle wearing a sundress without any underpants.

"So how did Treegate end?" Celeste asked.

"Lo and behold, Christmas went on," I marveled. My children avoided emotional scarring. I think."

"Sometimes we just need to cut ourselves some slack," Celeste nodded, as she picked up the sushi takeout boxes and made a show of tossing them in the trash.

CHAPTER TWENTY-THREE
Plan B

"He's off," I told Charlotte on the phone. By now, Sam would be settling into Caron, a treatment center in Philadelphia, at the forefront of addiction therapy.

"I wanted to be there, Mom. How did it go?"

"He looked at the floor most of the time, sweetie, with his head in his hands. I think he heard us though. You'll be there for him at Family Weekend. He'll be thinking more clearly then. I'm booking your plane ticket tomorrow."

The phone clicked. Maher was calling.

"Charlotte. Honey. Gotta take this call. It's the intervention guy. He'll have news about Sam. I'll call you tomorrow."

It was almost 10 p.m. I flashed over to Bill.

"Lynda, we've hit a snag…" he began, his voice sounded strained.

When haven't we hit a snag? I wanted to scream. Sam and snags are a two-for-one-deal. Why should I be surprised? What's the definition of insanity? Remind me again? Oh yeah, doing the same thing over and over and expecting a different result.

"Sam tried to light a cigarette during intake."

"A cigarette? Are you kidding me, Bill? Isn't that the least of our worries?"

Maher sighed, weary. "They've got a no-smoking policy. I explained that to Stuart when he picked the place. He said smoking's a nasty habit and the rule was probably for the best. Anyway, Sam would have no part of it. He wasn't staying if he couldn't smoke. No cigarettes. No rehab. He was emphatic, Lynda."

"So where is he now?"

"I've been on the phone with Stuart for the past hour, and we've got him booked at a place in Provo, Utah. Cirque Lodge. It's excellent—every bit as good as Caron, just not as convenient. Sam's agreed to give it thirty days. The flight leaves at 10:20 tonight and my DEA friend has promised me, he's not leaving Sam's side until he's buckled into his seat and the plane pulls away from the gate."

Maher and Stuart had jumped through hoops to locate a bed at Cirque and rebook Sam's ticket. I pictured a jet soaring mid-air, a vapor trail of shredded hundred dollar bills exploding behind it, like confetti from a cannon. After the two of us split seven thousand dollars for the intervention itself, Stuart went on to flush the cost of two plane tickets to Philly, purchased another at full fare to Salt Lake City, forfeited the deposit at Caron, and prepaid the stay at Cirque. I knew it wasn't easy for him. No matter what had gone on between us before, at the moment he was a rockstar in my book.

By now, the DEA agent was working overtime, his meter still running. At any price, a thirty-day program would barely scratch the surface for Sam. To get ahead of his snowballing drug abuse, he needed sixty to ninety days minimum, Maher had told us. But it didn't take a nationally renowned interventionist to figure that much out. Sam was in deep.

"Looks like that's our best bet right now, Bill. What a squirrelfuck. Jeez. The whole plan could have fallen apart. And Bill?"

"Yes?" he said, expectantly.

"Do you think?" I stammered, hesitating to heap more onto the burden he'd shouldered tonight. "Did we get through to him? I'm hopeful. But I don't know what to believe anymore."

He sighed. A desk drawer closed in the background.

"Anyway," I said quickly. "Can't thank you enough."

———

Cirque Lodge had an interesting history. Before it was transformed into a rehab facility, the main building housed the Osmond family's recording studio. Black accoustic panels lined the domed ceiling, hinting at the massive greatroom's past. In its heyday, the venue had been a destination for diehard fans of Donny, Marie and their six siblings.

The basic rooms commanded thirty thousand dollars a month. Up the hill, a deluxe room in Cirque's main lodge had a fifty thousand dollar price tag, which bought an additional security program to protect the privacy of celebrities, hedge-fund managers, and anybody else with really deep pockets.

When family weekend arrived, Stuart and I met Charlotte at the Salt Lake City airport and picked up the rental car for the short drive to Provo. We dropped our bags at the hotel, then headed over to see Sam, looking like a family again. Over the next five days, we'd peel back the layers to expose the wounds that had never been properly cleaned and dressed.

Key to the healing process—group tell-all sessions. Confession en masse. A spiritual exercise with strangers. I would rather have washed Stuart's feet. And everyone else's.

We pushed through the double doors at Cirque's main entrance, pausing to stomp the snow off our boots. And there he was. In his plaid, flannel shirt and Carhartt work pants, Sam looked like a true mountaineer. His color had returned; he grinned from ear to ear, overjoyed to see us. His good looks and charisma were precisely the same qualities that made him a successful drug dealer. The consummate host, he couldn't wait to introduce us to his new friends. From a middle-aged woman to a seventeen year old he called Hutch, he traipsed from person to person, talking about how good it felt to be clean and safe, in a place where he belonged, among amazing new friends and with the guidance of seasoned counselors.

"Dude, are these your parents?" A bearded fellow mountaineer named Ryan looked our way, while raising his palm to Sam for a high-five, as if to congratulate him on his extraordinary power of selection. He reached for Charlotte's hand first and shook it vigorously.

"And you're the sister he's been talking about. Charlotte, right?"

Rehab is one of life's great equalizers. We met all types that weekend. A tattooed kid, defiantly pierced, sat next to a cashmere blonde wearing expensive flats; his father, an L.A. music producer, conspicuous in his absence. Another fractured family. A son dying to be heard, seen, validated by a father who was wholly incapable.

Even with an outrageous monthly tab, Cirque's clients came from all rungs on the economic ladder. One couple, fresh off an Idaho dairy farm, looked terrified. As they settled into the Lodge's black and chrome folding chairs, I imagined their living room back home. A sofa with doilies pinned to the arms. An oak coffee table. A Bible displayed prominently. Beside them, a washed out girl with stringy hair sat silently seething.

Ryan explained that he'd be working with our three families, plus a lawyer from New York, whose wife, the executive director of a non-profit I couldn't quite get a handle on, had cut a conference short by one day to fly in for the weekend.

He motioned for us to arrange our chairs in a circle as he laid out the rules of engagement:

First names only.

No talking about jobs or careers during group.

Tell us why you're here and what you hope to gain from the weekend.

Ryan led a discussion that started with the biology of addiction: "No one can identify the specific gene or find the one switch that activates addictive behavior. But its there. Somewhere. We know that much."

"And if you ask an addict, what's your problem? The answer is never alcohol or drugs. That's what they use to medicate the underlying problem. They're numbing pain which is often rooted in shame and self-doubt."

I cringed to think of the heaping doses of both that Sam had absorbed from his earliest days in school. "The issues driving addiction are both biological and emotional," Ryan said before opening up to questions from the group.

Stuart listened intently, thoughtfully. Without the eye rolls, the fidgeting, the coiled-spring body language that predicted a walkout. He was fully present. After years of power struggles, denial, and divisive game playing, Stuart had arrived at Cirque with an open heart and mind. I sensed the clouds were parting, and we were standing in the warm sunshine, reading from the same well-lit page. He was trying hard. I remembered how I'd fallen in love with him in the first place.

The group moved on to trust games. I could have done without falling backwards into the dairy farmer's open arms. He probably felt the same way about catching all hundred and something pounds of me; which he did, with a quiet strength. I was grateful to be in safe company. We were no longer strangers. We were all in the same life raft.

———

Every night, after group, we'd drive back to the hotel, where Charlotte and I shared a room. Stuart's was next door. In many ways, we still *felt* like a family.

At nineteen, Charlotte was the youngest visitor that weekend and I worried about what she'd witness. When it was her turn to speak, she looked directly at Stuart and me. "You made it easy. And he's not stupid; he played you." Her voice was shaking but she caught herself, slowing down. "Just *talk*," she said softly. "Talk to each other. It shouldn't matter whether you're divorced. Do it for *his* sake." She went on to express the emotional impact that Sam's illness had had on her. And she rocked the house.

I'd been nervous about exposing Charlotte to the litany of disturbing stories that would be on parade over the course of family weekend. As she spoke, I saw a young woman I hadn't known before. I quietly wept with pride at the soulful, expressive person she'd become and it dawned on me that family weekend was just the platform Charlotte needed, a place to find her own voice and lift it—clear up to the acoustic panels on the Osmonds' ceiling.

"Siblings get a raw deal," Ryan said, pausing to let that thought sink in. "They grow up in chaos. Their parents are consumed with the addict's problems. The siblings avoid conflict at all costs. They don't dare rock the boat. And if they don't get counseling support, they'll spend the rest of their lives trying to rescue lost souls.

As we went around the group, each family telling their story, I discovered ours was no worse than anyone else's. But it sure as heck wasn't any better.

The old-fashioned model for recovery was thirty days of rehab— then phew! Glad that's over. Let's celebrate with a martini or a bong hit. But a week before Sam was due home, Ryan sent word that he'd committed to another thirty days. I was grateful for an extra month of relief. But no parent with a pulse should get too comfortable when an addict's involved. "Recovery is looking into that hole in the soul," David Sheff writes in *A Beautiful Boy*.

Twenty days in, Ryan called with the bad news. "We tried everything short of handcuffs. We begged him to move into a halfway house, at least," he reported.

I guess Sam got tired of looking into the hole in his soul.

"I know everything I need to know," he'd told Ryan, before he walked down to the highway and hitchhiked back to Colorado.

Ryan was dejected. "Sam has so much potential, but he wasn't willing to do the work to build the support network he'd need to see him through. I've seen it so many times: Once a kid starts getting their feet underneath them, they look around here and say, 'I don't need this shit anymore.' "

That was Sam. He had a million friends. But when push came to shove, he usually retreated and would try to go it alone.

"You tell Charlotte I was proud of her," Ryan continued. "I want her to hang in there. No matter what happens to Sam, this has been another building block to support his recovery. You tell her that. This time was not wasted. "

Sam had achieved compliance at Cirque, but he hadn't surrendered. Sobriety rooted in compliance won't last. Beneath compliance is the addict's idea that someday, they will be able to return to their drug of choice and figure out how to control it. Time after time, the addict's brain chemistry leads him down this primrose path.

Surrender, on the other hand, means the addict accepts the fact that addiction is bigger than they are. They are powerless to control it; therefore, they let go of the fantasy that they ever could. Grounded in the knowledge that managing addictive behavior is a lifelong process that takes the wholehearted support of a village, it is with surrender that the addict begins the active work of genuine recovery.

Hanging up the phone, my heart bled for Sam. He might have thought he was in control of things, but in reality, the disease held the ultimate power. His temporarily clean brain had seduced him into thinking he no longer required a vigilant recovery program. He had stepped away from his safety net, and had put himself in peril, all over again.

I pictured him standing on the highway waiting for an eighteen-wheeler to pull over and offer him a lift. He had no job in Colorado, no counseling in place, no group therapy sessions or sponsor who would have his back. The progress Sam had made at Cirque would quickly unravel. How would I break this news to Charlotte? She was entering her first round of exams. How could I pretend to be upbeat about his prospects?

Turned upside down, I was sure of only one thing: a backslide was probably in Sam's future. And mine.

CHAPTER TWENTY-FOUR
The Shark Who Stole Christmas

In every Southern city, the name of the psychiatric hospital flows through conversation like sweet tea at Sunday supper. "Lord, have mercy!" my grandmother would declare, pointing her perfectly manicured finger at my grandfather. "If you tell that worn-out-story one more time, I'm gonna wind up on *Bull Street*."

As any Columbia native can tell you, *Bull Street* was shorthand for the South Carolina State Lunatic Asylum—the last stop on the crazy train. "*Bull Street*, indeed," my aunts would nod knowingly, fanning themselves with church bulletins, ankles neatly crossed and tucked under their porch rockers. "She's right, Bully—my grandfather's football nickname—we're all gonna end up there, if you don't hush. Even we've heard that story a thousand times."

Now that the Asylum on Bull Street is a designated historic landmark, Columbia locals book their breakdowns at Werber Bryan. Upcountry in Greenville, my cousin Leslie might invoke Marshall Pickens. New Orleanians parade on over to *River Oaks*.

And in Richmond? It's *Tuckers.*

I checked in shortly after lunch on Christmas Eve.

———

"Dr. Buxton called us," the receptionist scowled. She handed me a clipboard. "Fill this out. Completely. Name, address, insurance company, date of birth, next of kin, reason you're here, medications." She continued to shuffle papers on her desk, not looking up.

I'd left Pat a desperate message. When I limped into her office the next morning, she met me at the door: *We're hoping you will consider a couple of days in Tuckers for observation. And rest, Lynda.*

Taking my hand, she led me back outside to the parking lot. Camille wheeled up, threw her Escalade into park, jumped down onto four-inch heels and trotted around to the passenger side. Her Himalayan lambswool vest tickled my arm as she guided me up into the front seat. With a family lunch in forty-nine minutes, Camille was all business. She fastened the seatbelt around me like I was a fragile child. Springing back into the driver's seat, she leaned over and patted my cheek. "You're doing the right thing," she said, before hitting the gas and high-tailing it over the James River Bridge.

Lanier and Amelia, poised at the revolving doors, pulled me out of the car and slammed the door, just in the nick of time, as Camille sped off. They each grabbed an elbow and shuffled me towards Intake. Sitting like three birds on a fence, me in the middle, they guided me through every tedious question on that damned clipboard. Once complete, we group hugged, and reluctantly, they turned me over to Nurse Ratched, who whisked me around the corner and out of sight.

When you enter a psychiatric hospital, even voluntarily, you can't check out until you're discharged by a doctor. I had no way of knowing when I'd go home. Ratched took me to the fourth floor, where we walked down a narrow hall through a series of doors. As each door closed behind me, I wondered when it would open again.

Behind the last set of doors, a nurse's station took center stage, surrounded by a large common area. I turned over my bag, and the admitting nurse rummaged through it like airport security.

If patients arriving at Tuckers weren't already depressed or anxious, the decor guaranteed they would be soon enough. The chairs and couches were empty, sagging like deflated soufflés discarded from a French restaurant. Alone in the corner stood a defeated, artificial Christmas tree.

I'd brought four shirts, one sock, nine pairs of underwear, three wool scarves, and some yoga pants. No bra. Makeup and contact lenses didn't even occur to me, but apparently, I'd felt a desire to floss—daily. Nestled in the side pocket was the ballerina-pink stuffed bunny Robert had given me one Valentine's Day, some aromatherapy hand lotion, and Dr. Kernoodle's book on panic disorders. My bag looked like a distracted third grader had packed it.

The nurse considered a ball of knitting yarn with two needles jammed in the middle. "We'll just keep these in here until group time," she said, nodding towards a metal locker. I wasn't trusted with knitting needles, and I didn't have the energy to protest.

I entered an empty room, praying I wouldn't have a roommate. I didn't have the strength to put on a "together face." But who in Tuckers was *together* anyway? My prayer went unanswered as a woman was wheeled in on a gurney from a round of electroshock therapy. As nurses helped her into bed, she sent a wan smile my way. I felt comforted by her gentle spirit. *Or was that the result of a jostled and electrified brain?* Whichever, we were two wounded birds who would share our healing nest together.

———

My best laid plans that Christmas hadn't included Tuckers. Robert and I had blended our families as well as anyone can in a mid-life remarriage, finally settling ourselves in the country, where we intended to entertain a group of fifteen on the night of the twenty-fourth. I was determined to create fun-family-and-friend-festivities in a new house that didn't yet feel like home.

Charlotte would be back from college. In a phone call from Colorado, Sam sounded upbeat. He assured me his job was rocking along, but he couldn't make it to Virginia for the holiday. I hadn't dared to ask what the "job" might be this time.

Since leaving Cirque, Sam had been cagey about his next steps. Lessons from the Family Program had been drilled into my head: *Sam's life is his responsibility. I can't nag, hen-peck, mother or smother this young man out of his addiction. And if I insist on doing it anyway? I'm part of the problem.*

———

I'd just spent two days at my Garden Club's annual greens workshop, gathering pine boughs, magnolia leaves and boxwood snippets—anything we could weave onto a frame with floral wire—to design our wreaths, garlands and kissing balls.

Twenty-two of us were in the creative zone. Giddy conversation rattled around the room as we twisted and tied: bouncing from talk of ham biscuits to grandchildren, Sunday School pageants to returning college-aged children. Who was coming for dinner? Who was serving turkey? Who'd ordered tenderloin? Long before the advertisers hijacked Christmas, Southern women—and probably Northern, too—have gathered to assemble Christmas garniture and share holiday gossip.

I checked my calendar daily, feeling a wee bit superior to the throngs of materialistic, spiritually-depleted people who commercialize this season a little more every year. My mantra was straight out of Dr. Seuss's *The Grinch Stole Christmas* and I absentmindedly repeated it throughout the weeks. "*It came without ribbons. It came without tags. It came without packages, boxes or bags. And he puzzled and puzzled 'till his puzzler was sore. Then the Grinch thought of something he hadn't before. What if Christmas, he thought, doesn't come from a store. What if Christmas, perhaps, means a little bit more.*"

I was rejoicing in authentic traditions, and my schedule was chock-a-block with cheer. Normally, I knew when to retreat from the social whirl, take a deep breath and a short winter's nap. But for the first time in months, we weren't living in the throes of a drug-related crisis. Liberated, I let myself get swept up in a celebration that had, so often for me, been one giant, red sourball. I'd earned this one.

Yes, this Christmas would be about fellowship, the Lessons and Carols Service at church, cooking and decking our halls with boughs of holly. I'd visit Mabel, our former housekeeper, and share the recent good news about my children with the woman who'd steadied me through some of our darkest days. I was jubilant. Or so I thought.

But in truth, I was the swimmer in the movie *Jaws*, paddling an inflatable raft out into the ocean, blissfully unaware of the great white shark lurking below.

As I wrapped presents a couple of days before the twenty-fifth, little did I know I'd have to be scraped off the floor and stuffed into a garbage bag like the scraps of colorful paper, empty rolls of scotch tape and bits of green ribbon scattered around me.

When the call came, I was scissoring through a length of wrapping paper, sitting in front of a roaring fire in our family room, surrounded by ribbons, tags, and bags.

"Hello."

Silence.

Strains of Whitney Houston's, *Do You Hear What I Hear?* reverberated from the ceiling speakers. Then I heard the click. A pause.

"You have a collect call from (pause) 'Sam', my son's voice dropped in between robo-phrases. "An inmate at the Adams County Correctional Facility."

I'd heard this before. It triggered a Pavlovian anxiety attack.

"To accept this call," the lady-robot went on, "from (pause) 'Sam', press one. If not, please hang up. Subject to Section 442869570 of the Colorado Penal Code, whatever you say will be held in accordance with..... blah, blah blah. The charge is $1.00 per minute."

I cleared the wrapping paper from my lap, struggled to stand, stiff from sitting Indian style, and scrambled to the kitchen to fish the credit card out of my wallet and punch in my account number. Another pause followed, then brrriiinnnggg!

"Hi, Mama."

"Hi, sweetie," I said, resigned to hear the same ol' story.

"Listen, here's the thing," he launched into the litany of excuses and explanations that protect him from the truth. This time, my heart didn't sink. Instead, blankness set in.

In jail. Out of jail. It had all started to feel the same.

The pattern had had me pin-balling between disappointment, outrage, compassion, and fear for years. But that day, I just felt drained. Flat. My emotional toolbox was empty. I had nothing left to offer him.

"They've set me up with a public defender," he continued. "And this guy knows it's all bogus. He's looked at my case. I can't talk long, Mama; I just wanted to say, I love you."

My imagination did a fine job of whipping up Sam's outrageous legal scenarios without his standard playlist of mitigating circumstances. A single night in jail often triggered a spate of imprisonments. By now, he'd probably been an inmate at least a dozen times. Sometimes for two weeks; other times for eight months. And, again, the news actually brought a perverse sense of calm. I knew where he was and that he probably wasn't using. I was slightly soothed but still morphing into a zombie.

"I love you, too." I answered, unsure of what else to say. I hung up the phone, scanned the fragments of Christmas spooling around me like a slinky and knew that, indeed, our holidays would be gathered up and tossed out along with them.

How would I tell my parents? Again?

What would my brother say? Again?

How could I entertain Christmas Eve guests when my son was behind bars in an orange jumpsuit? Again?

Could the timing be any shittier?

Pretending that all was calm, all was bright, when my own son, once again, got caught with the devil on his back, was not in my DNA. Were other women made of stronger stuff than me? Or did they also fear ap-

209

pearing vulnerable? Were other women *Steel Magnolia*s, who pushed their skeletons back in the closet and drawled out their southern "Merry Christmas, ya'll. Let's get together after the holidays!"

I couldn't keep a lid on it anymore. I wanted to wave the white flag and surrender, screaming, "I give up! I'm taking the season off. If anybody needs me, I'll be in my room eating TV dinners on a tray. But please don't anybody need me! Because, I might not surface until January."

———

Robert was working in Philadelphia. Alone that night, a blanket of dread draped over me and refused to let me sleep. Tossing it off like covers during a menopausal hot flash, didn't work. The next afternoon as I headed home from my appointed rounds, the dread teamed up with fear, confusion, anger, loneliness and sorrow and dragged them all into my soul with such ferocity that my knuckles turned chalk white as I gripped the steering wheel.

Terror took over.

Then sobbing.

Holy Mother of God, what the fuck was happening to me? My mother's words echoed in my head. "*Using that four letter word shows a lack of refinement, Lynda.*" Normally, I would agree with her. "I don't give a fuck about refinement right now!" I said aloud. *I want my son to get well. I want jolly and bright, sleep in heavenly peace. I want to create happy memories like my own mother did for me.*

I needed urgent help, but for what? I didn't know exactly what was wrong, or if I could tell anyone.

The panic I'd experienced years ago at my parents' house was making a return visit. My good friend and Robert's cousin, Kate, lived on the way home. I steered off the main road and peeled up her gravel driveway, praying she'd be there.

I rang the doorbell, agonizing over whether I should interrupt her at this busy time. After all it was one of the most hectic weeks of the entire year. But she seemed to be my only port in the storm. I trusted her to understand what I could not.

Kate happens to be a paramedic. Was I looking for medical advice? Was this some kind of illness? I prayed it was nothing more than a momentary imbalance. Later I would learn I was having another full-blown panic attack. But at the time, it felt like congestive heart failure or a stroke.

I now understand the suicidal impulse. I was seized by it that day. The idea of whipping my steering wheel into oncoming traffic seemed like the only way to get relief. It hurt so much to be me, right then. Suicide isn't so much about wanting to die, it's about needing to escape the pain of living. Death isn't the goal, it's just an unfortunate side-effect.

When Kate opened the door, she took one look at me and knew I wasn't there for a social visit. Tears sloshed down my cheeks, but I had no words to explain them. She put her arm around my waist, squeezed me with a knowing hug and guided me to her comfortable den. I was safe for the moment. There was that.

But I was still terrified. And the idea of talking about it felt like throwing gasoline on a fire. She offered me a cup of tea and a place to spend the night. I was too antsy to stay but too scared to leave. My skin was crawling.

Kate sat patiently, waiting until the panic subsided enough for me to speak. Then, she listened without judgement, never once implying she had anywhere else to be, anything else to do. Some people have that gift.

After an hour, I gathered myself to go home, fortified by her calm. A good night's sleep would cure this, wouldn't it? I couldn't tell anyone else; it was hard enough to find the words for Kate. I'd just have to strain forward. I was slowly falling apart and scared to admit it. I wouldn't tell Robert, either. If I distracted myself, maybe it would just go away.

I was playing whack-a-mole in my head. Each time I beat back one maniacal thought, another one reared its ugly head, wickedly grinning. The panic left me paralyzed, unable to think in the linear list-making fashion of the season.

Should I punt the ball, shift the dinner party for fifteen to my in-laws' house and cut myself some slack? Of course. Why not order up a basket of wings, a couple of pizzas, and a thirty-six inch sub? Not a snowball's chance in hell. I couldn't let go of the holiday nesting instinct. But before I could even try, it dropped me like a fickle friend.

CHAPTER TWENTY-FIVE
Every Woman's Fantasy

I wish I had a nickel for every woman I've met since then who's envied the Christmas I spent locked in Tuckers. The thought of letting go of teacher presents, ornament exchanges and the shopping-wrapping-cooking was tantalizing all by itself. When you factor in three meals a day served to you on a metal tray, Tuckers sounded like every woman's fantasy.

So there I was, living the dream.

Unpacking, I looked around, not sure how or where to settle in. Limp as Lucy the lamb, Charlotte's stuffed lovey, I curled up on my bed, with my back to the stranger and pulled up the thin blanket. I couldn't focus enough to read my book. My brain was shortcircuiting, and I was here for technical repairs. Years of yoga taught me how to tame monkey mind. I payed close attention to my breath, trying to clear the thoughts. I didn't have to put on a happy face anymore, and I felt relieved. I was handing over the keys, letting someone else take the wheel for a while.

Outside these walls, life went on. The dinner for fifteen shifted to my father-in-law's house. Trumpets carolled Glorias at the Christmas Eve service while our pew sat empty. Charlotte moved to her Dad's house. And on Christmas morning, Robert woke up alone. His boys were with their mother that year.

As I looked out my fourth-floor window on the twenty-fourth, I watched the hospital grounds crew blow leaves into neat piles, stuff them into bags and toss them into the back of open-bed trucks. From where I stood, the thick glass seemed to divide the world into two simple groups. Outside = business-as-usual. Inside = temporary insanity.

I remember thinking I was lucky. If I could just regain my equilibrium, I'd be back in my world in a flash. Like my roommate, most of my fellow inmates at Tuckers were suffering from long-term mental illnesses far worse than mine.

That first afternoon, when a male caseworker stopped by to conduct an evaluation, I thought: *He'll understand that I'm not like the others, those people are actually sick.* I'm just resting, just a little off my game. Surely my well-dressed caseworker would "get" this about me. Like a speedometer that was running too fast, I needed recalibration.

Med-trays came up throughout the day, and a nurse called names according to patients' schedules. With each dose, she scanned my hospital bracelet bar code, then the bottle of medicine. I did as I was told. Because I'm a rule-follower.

I'd been taking a controlled substance and, per doctor's orders, was supposed to follow a strict schedule; but I'd gotten reckless. I'd stopped taking my SSRI altogether, and I'd gotten sloppy about taking Klonapin, an anti-seizure drug that controls panic disorders. My psychiatrist Dr. Buxton—Pat's husband—had prescribed it, for the first time, a week earlier. I'd skip a day here and there or take my pill at night because I'd forgotten to take it in the morning. Withdrawal from Klonapin can bring on strong headaches and a floaty, disembodied feeling. Clearly, my brain was scrambled. And clearly, I was to blame. The visit to Tuckers was mandatory in order to get my medication back on track.

We had two hours of free time before dinner the first night, so I asked for my knitting. The nurse accessed my locker and handed it over, reminding me I'd have to stay in the common area. Hospital rules: "You can't take the needles back to your room."

Meals came on pre-loaded cafeteria trays and were delivered in an industrial cabinet on wheels. Patients gathered at a long table, next to my knitting circle, where staff members doled out the trays. I had no appetite, a sure sign that I was out-of-sorts, but sat down anyway, careful, aware that anything—a blank stare or babbling laughter— could trigger more anxiety.

I didn't chat with my neighbors because I didn't have the energy for other people's problems. And other than our problems, what would we talk about? I wasn't there to forge life-long friendships. How would I open a conversation anyway? *"So what brings you to Tuckers?"* I didn't much care what I looked like. And based on the prevalence of nap-squashed hair, bathrobes and sweatpants, it was clear nobody else did either. I was there to recover. That was enough.

After dinner, all who were ambulatory gathered for a mandatory breakout session. I shuffled into the lounge where, just like cliques in a high-school cafeteria, the longer-term patients took their seats with their friends. Newbies like me took the seats that were left. We stated our names and shared a fact or two about ourselves. "Hi, I'm Lynda." Pause. I searched for the right words, then simply settled on, "Anxiety."

I suffered through word association games, and short videos explaining mental illnesses like bi-polar disorder, schizophrenia, borderline personality disorder, and manic depression. At times the activities would even escalate my anxiety. Gradually I came to realize that these are life-long struggles, and even though my diagnosis wasn't as insidious as some others, I would be managing it for the duration.

Night ran on a strict agenda, just like day. I'd brought my own pillow; it had the comforting feel of home. I slept under the threadbare blanket, wearing my robe and socks, the weight of them keeping me anchored in bed. I hid behind the black screen of my closed eyelids, trying not to think. Outside my room, the red glow of the EXIT sign bounced off my door. The fourth floor clamored with hospital sounds: beeping monitors, rolling carts, nurses speaking in daytime voices.

Even the wee hours prompted an undercurrent of activity. Restless patients paced the halls, pressing the night nurse, "When is my next med check?" I'd hear a muffled response, then desperately, "Is there any way I can get it earlier?"

That first night, I hardly slept.

The next morning, I woke up so early, the birds were still asleep. The sun streamed through the plate glass window with the plastic mini-blinds, and I started the day hopeful I'd be discharged. I took my shower and ran a brush through my hair early in the morning, just to be ready when Dr. Buxton, *my* Dr. Buxton, got there. I wanted to look pulled to-gether, exactly like the kind of person who *didn't* belong in Tuckers.

I kept my eye on the doorway. It was Christmas Day. *He's probably not on call.* Still, I remained hopeful. I always felt sage with Dr. B and, right then, all I wanted was to see his compassionate face.

If you've never seen a psychiatrist, here's how it goes down: Your appointment is scheduled for fifteen, maybe twenty minutes. And you're not there to visit, unload or receive counseling. You're there for the prescription and to show the doctor that you haven't stopped bathing or started growing a pair of horns since your last appointment. His job is not to let the patient "unload" or talk about the past and what went wrong in third grade.

Buxton's job was to ask these questions:

"Are you jittery? Drowsy? Anxious?

"How and when do these conditions occur?"

"What outside factors affect your thoughts?"

And for me, the questions would include:

"Sam? How is he? Where is he? Is he still using?"

We'd hit the high points and the low points. And I'd try to give the right clues in exchange for the formula to regain my equilibrium: a prescription.

The phrase "mental illness" is a pretty big umbrella. I wouldn't think of myself as mentally ill, but the very definition of illness is the impairment of thought, mood or behavior. Your thoughts, feelings and actions are all affected. My diagnosis didn't stop at generalized anxiety. I was also experiencing "anticipatory anxiety." I was anxious about getting anxious again. The result is called "flooding." It's like a hundred cars hitting an intersection at the same time; no one knows who's got the right of way.

Dr. Buxton does not look like a psychiatrist. What ever that means. He looks like a football coach or an approachable movie star or someone you might like to marry. I'd been seeing him for the past few years, and we'd built a rapport. His wife was *my* Pat. Together the Buxtons saved my life; he wrote scripts while she listened, gently guiding me up and out of my darkness. Together they made a beautiful healing team.

For a lot of people, Christmas is a non-event, an ordinary day. And for the first time in my life, I was one of those people. I really didn't give a shit whether or not it was Christmas. I'd let go. With every fiber of my being, I had surrendered to my humanness. Unable to keep the plates spinning, I let them all wobble and crash to the floor.

Another doctor showed up late Christmas Day. He was not my doctor. Not my knight in shining armor. He walked in, glanced up and down a clipboard, then looked over his glasses at me.

"Dr. Buxton must be with his family today?" I managed.

"He'll be resuming his rounds tomorrow," the doctor offered, more focused on what he was scribbling on the clipboard. "It's up to him to assess."

I wanted to hear "You're all fixed; you can go home now." I wanted to curl up with my dog, Ginny, under my down comforter and get well from home. But he offered nothing, like the exhausted salesman in a department store who's worked too late on Black Friday.

I survived another night with the EXIT light shining in my face, taking little comfort in the fact that many of my floor-mates wouldn't go home tomorrow or the day after that.

When Dr. Buxton finally arrived the morning after, we withdrew to a little corner to talk. We settled into two crate chairs under that fucking EXIT sign and he asked about the last seventy-two hours.

Was I sleeping?

Was the medicine working?

How was the anxiety on a scale of 1-10?

He admonished me for weaning myself off the Klonapin. I was to never, ever take the administration of my medication into my own hands. *Did I understand that?* I promised to be good. We set a follow-up appointment for later that week. I'd earned my discharge.

Robert picked me up after the longest two and half days of my life. We met at the nurse's station to retrieve my bag. He wore the same helpless look I'd seen on men sitting in the OB's waiting room.

"I'll take your lead. Whatever you feel like doing is what we'll do," he offered.

The nurse turned the knitting needles over to me, proof that I'd graduated. As the stainless steel doors slid open, one after the other, clearing our path, freedom welcomed like a new day.

Homecoming was an exercise in more letting go.

"What are we having for dinner?" I asked, not thrilled at the prospect of food. I couldn't remember what was in the refrigerator, and I didn't care. I knew better than to jump back into the cook pit, anyway. Too soon. Robert sensed it, too.

I was still flat.

Robert was treading lightly, waiting for my cue, unsure what to make of this newly passive version of me. If I'd come home from the hospital with my leg in a cast, my sweet husband would have cheerfully fluffed pillows and placed everything within reach. At least once or twice. But this was tough. He didn't know how to help, and I was a lousy delegator.

Charlotte met us at the door and gave me a tentative hug, as if I were one of the glass angel ornaments my mother gave her every Christmas. Any moment, I might shatter into a million glittering fragments. If I'd ruined her Christmas, she wasn't letting on. Her face registered relief mixed with a hint of fear. She was old enough to show concern but too young to fathom the place where I'd been and the reasons that sent me there.

Christmas meant a freshly cut tree, pine garlands, a tenderloin, place cards, sweet potato biscuits, crème brûlée. The responsibility of creating happy memories fell squarely at my feet, dammit. I was determined to make everyone else happy, even if it killed me. Instead, I landed in the hospital, so I consider myself lucky.

I would learn later that my body's reaction, largely shock is ultimately a form of self-protection, even self-preservation. "Shock is a fabulous narcotic," writes Sorrel King in *Josie's Story*. "It can block the brain from sending damaging information to the heart and soul. It is a mechanism that protects us from feeling excruciating pain. In the face of crippling fear, pain or grief, the body releases endorphins, preventing the body from being overwhelmed, making it so the mind is unable to process the trauma all at once. Over time, the endorphin levels decrease, and the brain shifts the events into perspective." Only later would I put my time at Tuckers into such a logical frame of reference.

We spent the next week, quietly, as if I was getting over a touch of the flu. From time to time, Charlotte brought down the comforter from her room and flopped on the other sofa across from Ginny and me. She'd watch a movie, and Ginny and I would pretend to follow along.

A card arrived in the mail from Susan. I put the orchid from The Book Club on the front hall table. A member of The Greek Chorus wrote me a touching note.

By the time Charlotte left for school, I was making an effort to blow dry my hair and dot on a little lipstick. She could tell I was slowly on the mend.

"See? I knew you'd eventually feel better. You just needed to hang with me for a while."

In the quiet of January, I was wrapped in gauze, cocooning. Pat told me it would be important to embrace this time, to stay in the present moment, to heal, to be kind and gentle to myself. Maybe my meltdown had nothing to do with Sam going to jail. I was sorta used to that by now.

Or the new house. Or fifteen people coming for dinner. Maybe it was just the Klonapin. Who could say?

But my Christmas in Tuckers was a vacation, of sorts. For once, I didn't get in the middle of the holiday jam. And it was a present to myself.

CHAPTER TWENTY-SIX
Ghost Bully

Gingerly, the Book Club coaxed me back into the world. *Come over for a salad. Let's meet for a walk.* Robert and I shared suppers with devoted friends who treated my spell at Tuckers like any other hospitalization, asking openly what I needed. Others pretended not to notice. And how could I blame them? I moved through my days in a slow-motion lethargy tinged with dread.

I'm not sure what it truly feels like to be suicidal, by definition. There's a huge leap between *stop this ferris wheel so I can get off and I'm going to ride it to the tippytop and jump.* But for months after my Christmas in Tuckers, the idea of checking out crossed my mind. A time or two-hundred.

Dr. Buxton called these *passive* thoughts of suicide. It's junior level. Brownies to Girl Scouts. I didn't want to miss the rest of my life. Not really. I just wanted to skip the sucky parts. And right then, it was all sucky.

Pat spoke of rage. I protested at first. *Who me?* But the shattered career window, Charlotte's innocent angst, the terror, the defiance, the helplessness all come to a rolling boil and I sit with it. Searing, angry, hateful, I am pissed. I know that anger solves nothing, but I am enraged at the damage inflicted. The developmental delays. Tearful, furious, I look for something to punch. As if it would help. The tears purify somewhat, sweeping a hidden corner of my soul.

The undefined dread that shrouded my days and nights before Tuckers became more opaque in the months to come, a gray fog that swirled into a ghostlike form, taunting me for no particular reason. It trailed clammy fingers down my spine, dotted my skin with goosebumps, sabotaged my sleep, reduced my breath to small desperate sips, and deadened my senses, determined to take me down.

Often I'd think, *this is too much work*. And in those darkest hours of my sleepless nights, I'd craft the suicide script again, wearing my bamboo yoga pants and cotton tunic. Andrea Bocelli and Celine Dion on the radio. I'm in the garage with the car running. Nothing violent.

Whenever I fantasized about ending my pain—which was hourly—my rational self repeated a silent prayer, reminding my overwhelmed self to get a grip: *It would be tragic for Robert and Charlotte, if you took your life. Not to mention, Sam. Your parents and your brother would be crushed. Your friends would never let you hear the end of it. And might I add? Suicide would be a bummer for you, too, Lynda.*

I'd meet Dr. Buxton in his office each week, presenting a brave face. My wiring needed to be reset, so I'd no longer be a stranger to myself. "This takes time," he explained. "You must be vigilant about taking your meds, precisely as I prescribe. And continue your work with Pat."

As the pendulum swung from anxious twinges to full-blown panic attacks, my mind spun into worst-case-scenario mode: *Was Dr. Buxton even shooting straight with me, I wondered? What if I've hopelessly, irretrievably lost it? What if he just can't bear to report the full extent of the damage?*

I desperately wanted to get better, right on schedule. Put all this behind me. Check the box. Be a good patient. Make Dr. Buxton proud. I was determined to stay off of locked wards and keep my knitting needles, along with all my marbles. Still, it took an ocean of energy and a mountain of courage to make it to the end of each day.

I took on design jobs that spring, hoping to outrun the ghost bully with a flurry of busyness. But, still, I couldn't focus. I'd forget client appointments and more than once, I left a trailer full of plants parked in the hot sun to die.

Along with my work ethic, the ghost hijacked my ordinary pleasures. A darkened movie theater, once comforting, now felt cavernous and threatening. I recoiled at the touch of a massage therapist, the invasion unbearably intimate. And in my yoga practice, I panicked as the studio door closed and the temperature climbed to a hundred and two.

What was this silent bully? How did it know which buttons to push?

———

Our new house placed me twenty minutes from town. I was alone in the country. When I wasn't meeting with clients or friends, summer days were long and winter nights interminable.

Thank God for Ginny. She came from Shep, the proprietor of my favorite vegetable stand, who bred Cavalier King Charles Spaniels on the side. I was picking tomatoes from a bushel basket when I asked, tentatively, about his next litter. It just so happened that Shep's son, Charlie, was looking to place a three year old female "ruby" in a new home.

Shep's sales pitch was convincing. "She's a beautiful young lady, Mrs. Hatcher. Charming, housebroken, never met a stranger." We struck a deal.

It was love at first sight. Her cinnamon-colored coat and inquiring eyes melted my heart. Like Audrey Hepburn in *My Fair Lady*, however, she would need a proper hairstyle and pedicure. After a once-over by our vet, we brought her home.

Tyson, a neighbor's miniature pinscher, was first to press a call, tearing over the hill at full speed, barking like he owned the place. Polite but cool at first, Ginny grew fond of him in time. She loved exploring, but knew to cut a wide path around our neighbor's horses, scurrying home before I began to worry.

I'd never slept with a dog in my life. Until I met Ginny. Growing up, dogs were never allowed over the threshold of our kitchen door, much less on the furniture or, God forbid, in the bed. Now, I'm lulled to sleep by a symphony of snoring and a sonata of snorts.

When Robert was traveling and darkness fell early, Ginny sustained me. Her steadfast companionship mended my wounds and showed me what unconditional love can do for the human heart and soul. She doesn't have a degree in psychology or counseling. Her only license is a metal tag issued by Goochland County, Virginia, hanging from her pink collar.

Most nights, half an hour before bed, we'd sit in semi-darkness and meditate; Ginny draped over my lap or stretched out in the sliver between my hips and the arm of the club chair, keeping me warm, along with my favorite throw. I'd carry the conversation, her eyes responding with a silent dialogue of understanding. When life was especially unsettled, I'd ask her if everything would be alright, tears rolling down my cheeks and collecting on her fur.

The strain of living in emotional turmoil leaves scars. They tell us where we've been, but our scars don't have to dictate where we're going.

———

I was picking up groceries at the market across from Edith Goldman's office one day, when I struck up a conversation with one of the owners. *I know a little about flowers,* I found myself telling him, *and could he use some help in that department?* I gestured to an African violet which wilted on cue, as if to make my case. Before I knew it, I was filling out a W-2 and trying on a light blue button down no-iron shirt with Libbie Market embroidered on the pocket. I'd been hired.

I remembered that the author, Phyllis Theroux, entertains fantasies of running a register in a grocery checkout line. "Imagine the ego boost. People line up to see you. All. Day. Long."

I reported to work at six a.m. on Tuesday, Thursday and Fridays, leaving the house, and Ginny, in the pitch black dark. I manned the register. Delighted in the regulars who lined up to greet me. When I wasn't counting change, I filled napkin dispensers, whirled smoothies, and mastered the espresso machine, turning out double-shot, skinny, no-whip, hazelnut lattes with the assurance of a career barista.

On bakery duty days, I pulled hundreds of chocolate chip, macadamia nut, and oatmeal cookies from the commercial oven. I swept the floor. I took out the trash. And every two weeks, I took pride in my paycheck. It was small. But I'd worked hard. I'd earned it.

Libbie Market became my salvation. Part adult day-care for me, part occupational therapy, the store buzzed with purposeful activity, transporting me to a place where the ghost bully couldn't touch me. In the early days, it waited in the parking lot, leaning on my car, fingering a vaporous keychain.

But as months passed, the ghost bully returned only occasionally to remind me that it still wanted to call the shots. We settled into an uneasy truce. But as I began inching back into circulation, the ghost bully eventually skulked off, looking for someone else to pick on. The Book Club helped, as always. Celeste would breeze through my checkout line occasionally with nothing but a single onion on the belt, each time making me laugh anew.

I continued my search for a better balance. From chamomile tea to Kava, magnesium to melatonin, I tried it all. St. John's Wort might as well have been a TicTac, *as little as it helped*. I remained vigilant about my prescribed meds, just like Dr. Buxton advised. Thankfully, I'm back to where I started when it all hit the fan at forty—plus monthly B-12 shots, diatomaceous earth, and iodine drops twice a day. To discourage the ghost bully from taking an interest in me again, I cut out an extra evening glass of wine and trimmed my overstuffed to-do list.

Months later, when I found myself asking my manager to re-schedule my shift yet again, I took early retirement from the market. I left with a heavy heart, forever grateful for the job and to my colleagues. But my mother's health was deteriorating, and I was needed elsewhere.

CHAPTER TWENTY-SEVEN

All's Quiet (today)
on the Southwestern Front

The fresh, hip establishment was buzzing with the energy of weekday patrons. Sam took the bus from work and met me on the Sixteenth Street Mall, a well-known Denver shopping and dining area. He'd suggested the restaurant and texted the directions. His sister and her roommate, Kit, would meet us, after they returned from Whole Foods and put away their groceries.

The last time I saw him looking this sharp was, ironically, on the Christmas Eve of the broken arm and the Percocet haze. Today, he was crisp in a white button down shirt, a light blue patterned tie and khaki pants. He was beautifully, casually professional with a two-to-three-day beard and, for the first time, the haircut of a Colorado businessman, down around the collar.

I wrapped my arms around his neck and squeezed hard; he planted that familiar kiss right on my lips, only this time, there was a faint smell of tobacco. He's been a head-on kisser since he was a toddler and doesn't hold back when it comes to his mama. I love that about him.

He could have been anybody's polished young kid starting out at an ad agency or a dot-com. So striking, that had I seen him earlier on the mall, I would have done a double take. The blonde waitress, who later approached our table, seemed to notice, too. I was surprised and taken with his restaurant choice; we ordered our beverages and waited for the girls to arrive.

Our party of four enjoyed a delightful adult exchange for an hour and a half. Inherently funny and loaded with a healthier dialogue, Sam spoke with a lilting cadence. Absent was the reactive personality of the past. We had a balanced conversation. He told stories, but was just as intent to listen to ours and ask relevant questions. He was decidedly present and shared details of his job and impressive information about the city, which he had come to love.

For so long, he'd been mired in his own problems; today he was engaging with the world around him, offering his sister business leads, sure of the goings on about town, like a young professional. Taking an interest in the route that his sister had driven from Virginia—by herself, I might add – he checked on her the entire way.

I couldn't imagine a time in the past fifteen years that he might have joined us at a Thanksgiving meal to sit and shoot the breeze. Always fidgety, he'd pop up and down from the table, checking his cell phone, distracted. His uniform had been a hoodie and baggy khakis and that recognizable glaze in his eyes.

To the casual observer, today would have offered no indication of a struggle with addiction, much less chronic incarceration. Today, Sam looked confident and clean.

———

He had to be back at the halfway house by nine, so we said goodnight to the girls and walked back to my rental car. My hotel was nearby; I would drop him off on the way. Clouds gathered and night fell. As we drove back, conversation centered around his imminent release from the facility.

He explained that because of overcrowding, non-violent offenders may find themselves on an unexpected fast track. As his mother, my fear was that he was moving through the system too quickly. My hope was that prison would have slowed him down, gotten him in front of medical care and counseling.

Because he never got past the transitional diagnostic center, he never fell into that rhythm. I worried that he might not take the initiative towards consistent care, once he was in charge of his own life.

Pat's words washed over me, leaving a newly adopted sense of calm.

"Let go. He's a grown man. It's his journey. It's his karma."

We pulled up to the entrance of his cinder-block home. We planned to meet again the following evening after work. For the first time, in forever, I looked forward to our next visit.

CHAPTER TWENTY-EIGHT

Aha Moments in Cumberland Furnace, TN

I had the glass waiting room all to myself. But not for long.

As weary travelers drifted through the door into my space, I considered each, one by one, trying to figure out who might be booked on my shuttle.

Three women, filing in separately, wheeled their bags into a chosen safe area and sat quietly, not exchanging glances. There was a heaviness about them, a containment.

From my quiet corner, I heard one of them mention something about "a week with no phone." Bingo. I would spend the next six days with all three, bringing our lives back to center.

From the Nashville airport, I wasn't bee-lining for the Grand Ole Opry, but to a Living Centered Program called Onsite Workshops, in Cumberland Furnace, Tennessee. I was both relieved to have two hours before relinquishing my phone and computer for the week, and flat-out anxious about unplugging.

I spotted the Onsite shuttle pulling up to the curb. That was the cue to reveal myself. Gathering my belongings, I made my way to the van, along with the three female suspects. Handing Shamu (what my husband calls my bulky, more-appropriate-for-a-college-student, roller duffle) to the driver, I took a back row seat, wiggling in between a tall, handsome man and a petite woman with the face of an angel.

After exchanging pleasantries, I pulled out my phone, nervously checking texts and emails. As we drove an hour through the rolling countryside, I felt the weight of apprehension. At last, the shuttle crunched up the long driveway to a stately Victorian house, greeted by a four-dog welcoming committee. With sweaty fingers, I sent my husband a quick text that I'd arrived safely and would call him in a week.

—

"The Living Centered Program is Onsite's core program. It's designed to help you bring your life back to center. Often life events, relationships, trauma, distorted or compulsive behaviors in yourself and those you love, depression, anxiety, codependency or the stresses of daily living can keep you from the peace and balance you desire. LCP has, at its foundation, an experiential group process supplemented by education and action for change. The first days of the program focus on the importance of knowing yourself, how you have become blocked from being all you can be, how you may avoid looking at yourself and how the sum of your past experiences may be affecting you today."

After dinner, Bill Lokey, Onsite's Clinical Director welcomed us. "This week is about you. You're here to do individual work in a group setting. This is not about measured results. It's about our leaders sharing a broader perspective and giving you more tools to do *your* work. What each of you takes away is going to be very different. We're here to walk the walk with you because we've all done it ourselves. While some of you may be dealing with overwhelming life issues, others have come to get in touch with your own hearts. Onsite isn't a faith-based program, but many who attend are seeking a higher level of spirituality. It's truly open to anyone who wishes to grow."

Every day, every meditation, every lecture, every small group session, every delicious meal, every action-packed evening activity was filled with aha moments. Some participants say that six days at Onsite is the equivalent of eight to twelve months of therapy. It's difficult to quantify enlightenment, but that sounds about right to me.

———

My week at Onsite was, without question, transformative. Our group of forty strong had traveled a great distance since opening night. We came with vastly different stories but at the end of the day, we realized our basic human needs: to be heard, to be held, to be comforted, to feel safe, to be validated and to be loved.

I was ready to get back to my life. My new friends would go back there with me in my heart.

CHAPTER TWENTY-NINE
My Bruised Orange Soul

Accumulated heartache takes up residence inside our bodies where it grieves, rages, despairs. Mine moves around like a restless college drop-out before curling up and settling in the hollow below my ribs. Yours might ignite a skin rash, thrum migraines into your temples, or knife you in the back. The body speaks for the soul and mine was howling to be heard.

The dull ache confounds a chiropractor, an orthopedist, and a gastroenterologist. Two CAT scans, two endoscopies, a HIDA Scan, X-rays of the thoracic spine, and a gastric motility test come back negative. Still, the pain persists. I can't help conjuring the six-letter C-word. This must be the punishment I deserve for taking up for myself.

Acupuncture helps calm the meridians but my doctor isn't satisfied. He wants an answer as badly as I do. As he studies another set of test results—all negative—he taps his pen on his I-Pad, thinking, thinking, thinking until…a lightbulb.

"You know where this pain is, don't you?"

"Of course I know!" I flatten my palm like I'm offering a handshake, then turn it inward, pressing my fingertips into the space where the flat, hard sternum gives way to soft belly. "It's right here, where my bra hits my ribcage." I make this odd hand gesture so often now, friends have commented. The ache pulsates, knocking, like something's trapped inside, desperate to get out.

"No, that's not what I mean." My sweet, white-lab-coat wearing M.D. smiles.

"Then where is it?"

"It's your solar plexus." The solar plexus, located in the abdomen, is the seat of the third chakra, a beacon of light radiating from the center of the body. The third chakra is where your self-esteem sits. It's message is loud and clear. You have willpower. And you have the power to choose.

I look back at him, expectant. "And?"

Thoroughly steeped in Western medicine, my doctor takes off his glasses and looks at me through kind eyes. "Lynda. That's the seat of your soul."

———

"What are you poking at?" My friend Robin is fascinated with energy healing. While reconnecting at a dinner party, she's noticed my belly-pressing gesture.

"Oh this? I've seen doctors. Nobody can tell me." I wave her off.

Still, Robin persists. "Right there?" She points to my pain and registers understanding. "That's your third chakra, Lynda. It's your voice. Your power. *Your will.*"

"What power?" I said, half-kidding.

"You've got something to say and you need to be heard. That's the source of your pain. Your body's speaking up, it's making your silence uncomfortable, pressing you to shout it from the rooftops." She says all of this matter-of-factly, like duh any third grader knows that.

The seat of my soul was crying out for attention. And the answers I needed were falling right into my path. I wrote down the number Robin plucked from her phone.

"Kimmee," she explained. "She's a medical intuitive and massage therapist. She'll see it. She'll know."

A week later I walked into Kimmee's office, a comforting space lifted straight from the cardboard pages of *Goodnight Moon*. When she emerges to greet me, I half expect her to offer milk and cookies with a nap mat.

"Oooooo, Lovebug," she says, holding up her hands as if shielding her eyes from a blinding light. "I'm seeing orange," she circles her palm over my chest and belly, "and it's coming from right there." She stands back to assess, looking me up and down. "Inflammation. We've got to calm that down. It's not red yet, thank goodness. But it's mad as hell."

I take in Kimmee's fiery hair and warm authority as she fits clean flannel sheets over a massage table. I just know she's an angel.

"What happens when it turns red?"

"Girlfriend, it's like this. Yellow is mild irritation. Orange means you're on a crash course. Red is *Holy Shit!*"

She pauses, patting the massage table, inviting me to lie down. I slide under the top sheet and fuzzy blanket, as Kimmee positions the bolster comfortably under my knees.

"We all have an energy field surrounding our bodies," she continues, softly. "And when there's unresolved emotion, that energy field picks up a negative charge. So the orange light that covers your midsection? That's emotional debris clinging to you. We need to clear the channels before it turns red."

Kimmee scans the ceiling, like she's listening for clues. She and I have never laid eyes on each other before today. She knows nothing about me. Robin hasn't mentioned me to her, either.

"I'm getting something about a child. A boy?" she says, as if she's tuned into a radio station. "I see a lot of sadness. You've been carrying this for a long, long time, haven't you?"

Tears rolled over my cheekbones and puddled in my ears. Kimmee was peering directly into my bruised orange soul.

"Your body takes in and records emotional and physical assault. Some people are particularly empathic—they pick up pain in others, and they hold onto it. We all have that capability. It's just a matter of whether we choose to tune in."

"The seat of our soul is like a screen door," she explains. "Emotional energy should swirl out as easily as it flows in. That way, we can tend to other's pain and show compassion, but the pain doesn't gain squatter's rights. It doesn't stick to us, gumming up our own emotional filters. That screen door is there to let others in but to keep their baggage on the front porch."

"Looks like mine's missing the screen."

"That's right, honey. And you've got a sheet of fly-paper hanging right where that screen should be—with a welcome mat to boot. Everybody else's emotional junk has swarmed right on in and gotten stuck. Honey, you are weighed down with everybody else's dead flies.

"And then there's you. I'm sensing disappointments. A relationship in conflict. And I'm getting the letter S. Does that letter mean anything to you?"

CHAPTER THIRTY
Grace and the Green Dot

In her memoir *It's Always Something*, legendary comedienne and Saturday Night Live star Gilda Radner says, "*I wanted a perfect ending. Now I've learned, the hard way, that some poems don't rhyme, and some stories don't have a clear beginning, middle and end.*"

God knows, it's tempting to embroider a perfect ending right about now. I wish I could tell you that *Sam's living a productive, sober life in full recovery. I'd add that I'm 100% gluten-free, exercise religiously and wake at five every morning to meditate. Stuart and I have kissed and made up. And Charlotte? She hardly remembers the unpleasantness. In fact, our holidays are one big love-fest, holding hands and singing to the top of our lungs, like the Whos in Whoville.*

But you and I both know better.

Sam was on track for a while after our promising dinner at the hip Denver restaurant. Then, he relapsed. Then, he relapsed again. He was in and out of jail as often as my mother was in and out of the hospital.

One Easter, she landed on the fourth floor at Greenville Memorial while my father turned up on three, in ICU. A "cardiac event" had knocked him off his feet in the driveway, keys in hand. His head left a dent in the car door, like a signature, as he collapsed onto the pavement, fracturing a vertebra.

My brother and I spent Holy Week yo-yoing in the hospital elevator, taking turns with each patient. We bent straws to their lips, met with specialists, and delivered the cryptic messages that only a couple with fifty-seven years between them could understand.

After my mother's vascular dementia diagnosis, my father was her chief care-coordinator. From his bed in ICU, he anguished at not being by her side. My mother took comfort in news of his progress. She had a vague idea of what was going on. And that was reassuring. "But there'll be a day when she doesn't," my brother John gently reminded me. "It's coming, Lynda."

To cope, I chanted my homemade mantra: Somewhere in this madness, let me find gratitude and grace. I caught myself wondering how I would manage multiple, cluster-you-know-whats—all at once. Suppose my mother was rushed to the ER *again*, Charlotte broke up with a boyfriend *again*, and I received a jailhouse robo-call *again*, all in the same week? I pictured cars careening through a four-way stop and crashing in a tangle of metal and glass.

"Do the best you can, Lynda," my mother has preached all my life. "That's all anyone can ask."

I've heard it, studied it, debated it, challenged it, fought it, and what-if'd my mother's wise words. But it wasn't until Pat showed me how to live it that I began to know, for a fact, my mother spoke the gospel truth.

My paranoia is tempered by a newfound conviction. When I catch myself spooling out the cotton candy story, I picture Pat clasping her hands together like she's just caught that lightning bug. "Let's hold those thoughts," she'd suggested on the first day we met.

I picture a wave washing onto the beach. When the foamy edge has stretched as high as it can go, it pauses before folding back on itself and retreating into the ocean. That moment, when the wave hangs suspended, reminds me to take a breath.

Besides, crisis or no crisis, our grass needs cutting; my password needs resetting; the septic field needs pumping; the church committee meets on Friday, the weeds in my garden are winning, and the check-engine light is on—*again*. Always something. Always will be.

———

When the Sam-shaped hole in my heart aches, I scroll through his Facebook page, stealing a glimpse inside his world. I find him and his black lab, Lily, smiling for the camera. Soulmates. A girlfriend dancing barefoot in a tank top and flowy skirt, a long braid trailing down her back. An outdoor concert. A Colorado Easter service at Redrocks. In every frame, he looks like a man who's got the world on a string. I often work up the nerve to check his private message status. My heart flutters when the green dot is lit. But more often than not, it sits dormant and gray. I fear this means more jail time.

As he turns thirty, Sam knows that drugs have brought him a life of pain and punishment. Better than anyone, he knows. And when he's ready to wake up—and not a moment before—he will do what he's needed to do all along.

But how am I supposed to enjoy my life when my child's life is scratched, dented and misshapen? How does this serve him or me? If I spend time in-

vesting in my own emotional health, does it mean that as a mother I'm giving up on my son?

I lose contact with him, off and on, often for months at a time. Another Thanksgiving will come, and most likely he won't be at our table. I've accepted this. He may never know the joy of being a father or of finding passion in his work. It pains me, but I'm accepting that, too. Over time, these harsh truths have been woven into the fabric of our family life. Like a fiberglass blanket, this reality looks soft, but it stings and cuts when least expected.

Through it all, Sam falls in love. He goes back to jail. His dog, Lily, goes to live with his sister or a friend for a couple of weeks or months. He's released. He picks up Lily, starts a new job, falls out of love. He uses again, gets busted, goes back to jail. Lather, rinse, repeat.

"To interrupt a pattern that's not working, you have to be conscious and awake," Pat reminds me. We're all human; all flawed. Still, we are tasked with our own awakening. The process requires us to peel back the layers.

We might possess a strength in physics and a weakness for cheeseburgers. The shy gentle nature that earned us gold stars in grade school might mask a hair-trigger temper in adulthood. If we're fully awake though, we learn to accept ourselves as we are, not only as we wish to be.

We work to smooth our own rough edges. And when we can acknowledge our failings while recognizing our worth, we slip into our own skin and inhabit it comfortably. Like the Velveteen Rabbit, we become real. We live and love in our truth.

If only I could tell Sam all of this.

———

Life for others moves forward. I can celebrate their joys now without making comparisons. My heart swells at weddings. I delight at christenings. I send gifts honoring graduates. I quietly weep at funerals and when yet another hospital trip stretches to ten days, I draft my mother's obituary, just in case, knowing that I haven't cornered the market on this particular brand of suck. Joy and heartbreak, life and death, light and darkness. You can't have one without the other. That's the deal.

My own awakening has been tangled up in *Motherlove*. It's taken years, but I'm no longer the woman who'd hesitate to lock the front door and turn off the porch light. I pray Sam will find a healthy coordinate on the map of his life. Somewhere between prison and priesthood would be nice.

On Book Club nights, as we clean up after dinner, I notice that I'd rather tidy up a friend's kitchen than my own. Other people's messes are always more interesting. "Don't you worry about Marshall," my friend with twins admonishes, when one boy tattles on the other. "You just worry about Jack. That's a full time job."

The theologian Frederich Buechner puts it more elegantly: "Stop trying to protect and rescue, to judge and manage the lives around you," he writes. "...the lives of others are not your business; they are God's business."

I take comfort in this wisdom and forgive myself as I wipe Celeste's countertop clean.

CHAPTER THIRTY-ONE
Four-Way Pileup

Just as I'd predicted, the traffic light short-circuited and the cars piled up smack in the middle of the intersection.

Another.

Great.

Big.

Clusterfuck.

Oddly enough, this one began in an effort to simplify.

Our house in the country had become a endless list of to-dos. For every two items I'd strike through at the top of my list, I'd add six to the bottom. I was blessed to live where deer sauntered past the kitchen window as I sipped my morning coffee. I'd grown attached to the red fox, who popped up from behind the board-and-batten barn, in a game of peek-a-boo we'd fallen into over the years. I'd found comfort in the sound of neighbors on horseback clopping along the ridge, silhouetted in the western afternoon sky. When the horses stopped to graze, my neighbors would call out and wave.

I felt a childlike anticipation when the hummingbirds arrived on schedule, to dip their long noses into my favorite mexican salvia, "Black-and-Blue," and announce the arrival of summer. And I'd grown accustomed to Ginny's gentleman friend, Tyson. A miniature pinscher, he crossed the pasture to press a call, nearly every afternoon. As he trotted up the driveway, she would prick up her ears and scamper off the front porch, pausing to greet him with a flirtatious tail-wag before the two fell into a butt-sniffing circle dance.

But more often now, I was leaving. Locking the house hurriedly and rushing out of town. If I wasn't hitting the highway to check on my parents, I was joining Robert on a business trip, organizing pop-up road-shows where I sold Turkish and Moroccan rugs out of cavernous warehouses up and down the East Coast, or shuttling down to help Charlotte in Charleston as she set up her newest apartment.

My house and I weren't nurturing each other any more. I had quietly dropped the hint to our realtor-and-Robert's-cousin Kate. If she put the word out and kept it on the down-low, we'd entertain a buyer. Robert wasn't close to all-in with this moving thing, but eventually he gave in, knowing it made way too much sense.

Ask and it shall be given. The first couple Kate ushered through the door had been looking high and low in our neck-of-the-woods for months. One week later she delivered a contract. Suddenly, we were forced to make the next monumental decision. *Where the hell do we go now?*

My friend Cameron calls Parkside Place, "The Glue Factory," "Who are you kidding? It's where the middle age-ed are put out to pasture." Hmmm. But we really, truly didn't want a lawn to mow, a basement to flood, or an aging roof to re-shingle! The Parkside brochure rhapsodised about "lock and leave" living. And the kicker was the garage. Once you pulled in and hit the remote, the door slid to a close, your car safely hidden. We'd enjoyed our peace and quiet in the country. Now, we could have our cake and eat it, too. Friends around the corner, hip restaurants on the Uber route and, thanks to the garage, privacy assured. In four days, it was ours.

I can handle this. The move will be horrendous, but once we're situated at the Glue Factory, life will be less complicated. I'll be better prepared to respond to a crisis-call from Greenville and maybe even get some more exercise. I'm simplifying, I tell myself. *I'm streamlining. I'm letting go of excess baggage, not to mention an awful lot of shoes and the good china from my first marriage.*

I know how stuff multiplies, from coat-hangers to errands. And I'd vowed to tackle the house systematically. Each weekend, Robert would come home to find another room stripped bare. "Where did you put the table?" he asked, when confronted by an empty dining room. "Weren't we having the neighbors for a farewell dinner?"

In a flurry of goodbyes, I'd visit those neighbors bestowing gifts of rakes, extra garden-hoses, a hedge-trimmer, organic insecticide, and a leaf-blower. Other odds and ends went to our local tree-guy. We re-homed two grills with Kate and her brother. And I discovered that I would get along perfectly well, thank you, without a push mower or a nineteen-minute drive into town every day.

Just weeks until closing, I continued my work, room by room, sending more furniture into storage, stirring paint in a waxy paper cup to touch-up trim. I had a schedule and a game plan that kept the anxiety at bay. But an emergency call from my father sent me reeling.

My mother had broken her hip. We all knew it was coming. A partial hip-replacement was her only chance of walking again. If the truth be known, it was her only hope for survival. Over the last seven weeks, I'd made the six-and-a-half hour drive to South Carolina four times. This would make number five.

Back to Richmond, I touched base daily with my father by phone. I'd pack a few more boxes. Touch up some more trim. Then I'd toss one or two items into my overnight bag. At any moment, I'd need to go *again*. There'd be little extra time to pack.

The surgery had left mom with a life-threatening infection. As a result, she transitioned into hospice care. Every other day, Cynthia, her hospice nurse, would call with updates. "It's not time," she'd reassure. "We can usually predict within a day or so. Your mother will let us know. She'll tell us. There are clear signs and I'm not seeing them quite yet. You focus on your move. We've got this, for now."

With less than a week to go, I was marshalling the best of Pat's wisdom:

"Don't get overwhelmed by the big picture."

"Break it into small bites."

"Pace yourself."

"Don't panic."

"Ask for help. *Hire* help. Its money well spent. Its your family, not the stuff, that matters right now."

Moving day was scheduled for Friday. Again, I channelled Pat. Peace. Positivity. Deeeep breathing. This too shall pass. Keep the end-goal in mind and don't get caught up in the story.

———

Sunday morning, I dialed my Dad's number.

"Lynda?" my father sounded deflated. "I don't know how your mother made it through last night," he launched in. "I've told her goodbye three times."

I survey the room: Neat rows of boxes, stacks of books, the vacuum cleaner trailing its hose, a row of decapitated lamps, their shades carefully bubble-wrapped.

"...breathing is labored. Every hour, I'm here to tell you, we're seeing her decline."

Then he catches himself, adding, "But I know you've got so much on your plate right now."

"Last night?" I say, stupidly.

"I don't know how to advise you," he says, finally.

Like a pregnant woman whose water has just broken, I grabbed the bags I'd been living out of. Yoga pants for long hospital spells. A navy funeral dress, because you never know when. My not-too-sexy-not-too-conservative funeral shoes. It was time. And I knew it.

Robert was knee-deep in a thorny negotiation at work. I hurried down the hall to his home office and pushed through the door without a courtesy knock. "I've got to go."

"Go where?" he said, looking up from a stack of papers he'd been weeding through, as if I might be popping out for a smoothie.

"Home. To Greenville. Mom's fading fast. I think this is it."

As soon as I cleared the on-ramp towards 85-South, I dialed her cell and left a message. "Kate, I've run out of options. I'm headed to Greenville. We've got to call in reinforcement. Bonnie, my housekeeper can help. We'll manage the whole thing by phone. We can handle this. We're almost there." I willed my heart rate to slow down as the words spilled out in a deliberate, staccato stream of trying to plan ahead.

When the sun wakes me Tuesday morning in my parents' house, I'm shocked that I've managed to sleep through the night. I tiptoe downstairs to find my brother at the kitchen table, reading the newspaper on his iPad. "I'm texting Cynthia," I tell him, skipping good morning. *Did you sleep well?* "Mom isn't letting go, for whatever reason. So how about you and I give Dad the morning off? We'll go out to see her together."

All three of us had given my mother permission to leave us, over and over again. "Maybe she doesn't want to let go in front of Dad. Maybe you and I should have a little talk with her, just the two of us. Maybe she needs some more encouragement. Maybe, I need to have a little talk with Cynthia. By myself." My brother looked at me like, *What are you up to?*

I sent the message. Then added: "How can we let Mom know it's okay?" Cynthia sent a wink emoji in reply. *Got it. See you at ten.*

———

I poked my head in the door to signal that we'd be waiting down the hall. Cynthia was already by our mother's side taking vitals when we arrived. The room felt peaceful.

John and I headed toward some comfortable chairs. We'd taken about ten steps down the hall when Cynthia appeared through the doorway and trotted after us. "I think she's passing," "Heart rate's low. Come sit with her," she made a welcoming gesture. "It won't be long, now."

You don't mess with Cynthia. She'd ushered many of Greenville's finest out of this world. Her assured authority made me wonder if anyone ever dared to die before Cynthia gave the nod. She knew what she was doing and today, as in every other day, she was clearly in charge.

Because of her infection, we had to "glove and gown up" before entering Mom's room. "It's showtime," I say to my brother, a statement I make regularly when facing a challenge. We give our gloves a final snap, tie our gowns in the back, and trot behind Cynthia like obedient children. As we take our places on either side of our mother's bed, Cynthia whispers, "I'm here now. I'm not leaving." She settles into the recliner in the corner. A sign of her skill, she knew when to make herself invisible.

We listened to the rhythm of her breath as our mother pulled air into her lungs with stubborn determination. Cynthia had made sure she was comfortable. I couldn't help connecting the process of dying with labor and delivery. The two, like bookends, coming and going, guided by breath.

John and I each took a hand. And over the next forty-five minutes, we held on tight. We kissed her forehead. We told her we loved her. We timed each breath as they spaced farther and farther apart. We laughed. We cried. We commented on her stubbornness—and ours.

We told her we'd take good care of Dad. And we reminded her that she'd taken Holy Communion and spoken with each of her grandchildren. Even Sam had received special permission to call from jail in Denver. She'd listened graciously as he told her goodbye.

I joked about how her mother must be shuffling the cards, ready to deal her into a game of heavenly bridge. And her father and brother would be ready with their stories. Their wit could have matched any stand-up routine. "Bully's up there telling that same old worn-out story, remember, Mom?"

We count 15 to 20 seconds between breaths. After each one, we wait. My brother's eyes meet mine. After a pause stretches to 30, we swivel our heads toward Cynthia. She looks up from the notepad in her lap, meets our gaze, and silently nods, left to right. Not yet.

On cue, mom gasps. Then, a pause. Profound, *excruciating* silence. Her hazel eyes open for the first time in five days. Her gaze floats towards the sky. I reach across her body with my free hand to grab my brother's. This time, the staccato exhale feels deep and slow and bottomless. Then nothing.

Cynthia nods and stands. Reaching for her stethoscope, she positions the earpieces. "Let me check," she mouths, barely audible. Bending over mom, she gently positions the chest piece. And listens. Then pulls the stethoscope from her ears and looks lovingly at her patient's children.

"She's gone."

I still have one hand holding tight to mom, the other clasping my brother's. I lay my forehead down on his hand, squeezing it with all my might. As I exhale a ragged sob, I feel the warmth leave her body.

I look up at my only sibling, emotionally cross-eyed.

"Would you mind calling Dad?"

CHAPTER THIRTY-TWO

You Must Wonder

Why would I commit my story to paper, bind it up in a book, and ship it out for God knows who-all to see? What would possess me to share my most shameful memories? I'm not proud of losing my religion with my fifth grader. Why resurrect the death of my first marriage? Why tell of my Christmas spent on a psych ward? These snapshots hardly flatter.

"You must wonder why I tell it at all," Robert Goolrick writes in his memoir, *The End of the World as We Know It.* "You must wonder at the selfishness, at the hurt inflicted, at the terrible aches revisited for no real reason."

I tell it for the invisible casualties of addiction: The mothers who held their perfect newborns and cried grateful tears. Who plucked wakeful toddlers from their cribs at three in the morning, wrapped them in blankets, and tiptoed downstairs to snuggle on the sofa until they fell back to sleep. *How did we get here from there? We put heart and soul into mothering. Where did we fail?*

I tell it for all the young, innocent couples in this ever-changing world who have sweet dreams of starting their own family.

I tell it for those who have never seen the underbelly of addiction.

I tell it for the parents who've been robbed of the joy of seeing a child turn a passion into his life's work. I tell it so that those parents are not robbed of their own lives, as well.

I tell it because I have crossed the street more than once to avoid a well-meaning friend. I'm sorry. I just didn't have the strength, not that day, to muster a smile and change the subject when you inquired, always with kindness, about Sam.

I tell it because, on bad days, a Doubting Thomas still drags an aluminum lawn chair into my consciousness and settles in. And whenever he's feeling particularly passive-aggressive, or maybe just bored, he'll look up from clipping his ragged nails and call smugly over his shoulder: *Are you sure you did all you could? Was there an expert you overlooked? A nugget of wisdom you failed to convey?* He'll shift in his chair and add, *Didn't you order a book about this?* Then he'll pause and scratch his hairy potbelly under his wife beater t-shirt: *Just wondering.*

I tell it because I still grieve the son I do not know. "It is easier to look at death than it is to look at pain," Goolrick continues. "Because while death is irrevocable and the grief will lessen in time, pain is too often merely relentless and irreversible." At times, I've thought death—mine or Sam's—would have been preferable. With death, at least, you get closure. And a nice going-away party.

I tell it for the parents who struggle with the hard conversations. Whether their marriage is intact or in shambles, I wish them the gift of cooperation for the sake of their family.

I tell it for the mother who has not laid eyes on her first born child in almost four years. Who cannot picture where he lays his head at night. Who longs to send a funny card or a letter of encouragement, if only she had an address. Who has not one name or cell number of her son's friends, in case of an emergency.

I tell it because addiction kills. Overdoses come with the territory. For the lucky ones, they're just close calls.

I tell it because I love my son with all my heart and with all my soul and I pray that his story does have a happy ending.

I tell it for the Greek Chorus and the Onlookers, that they may find compassion. For we cannot know what goes on behind closed doors, even those flanked by wrought-iron planters that bloom with impatiens and pansies.

I tell it for all the teachers who lived and breathed and gave their all to strong-willed children like mine for eight hours a day and wonder how some of them turned out.

I tell it for every parent who dared to issue a strong warning earlier tonight and who now paces the floor, feeling weak and small and scared as the clock on the kitchen wall ticks past curfew. They know it's time to turn off the porch light and lock the front door. Still, they hesitate. I tell it because they *must* do this.

I tell it for the sisters and brothers. They are the collateral damage. They have sacrificed more than we know as they live in a world where their addict-sibling is also an energy vampire.

I tell it for the parent who opens his or her checkbook hoping that, this time money will buy a solution.

I tell it for the addict who is so tangled up in the legal system that he can't find his way back to a fresh start. There are support services available to help you put one foot in front of the other. Find your way into any church, AA or NA meeting and ask for help. You *must* do this.

I tell it for the parent who's frightened of the child they love. You are not alone.

I tell it for the countless hours, weeks, and years I spent in church basement Al-Anon meetings, drinking cold coffee from styrofoam cups and, later, reading Melody Beattie with the Book Club, so that someday I might heal for the people I love; the people who need me and who love me back. I'm not willing to let addiction win. Twice.

I tell it because it would be selfish not to share Pat's healing wisdom. She's too damn good to keep to myself. Through her, I found a voice and the courage to use it. A voice to empower myself and to encourage others to no longer deny their story, but to *own* it.

I tell it to reassure anyone who needs to hear it that, somewhere out there, a caring professional is willing to sit with you in your pain. And when you're feeling strong enough, that same someone will stand by you as you take your first wobbly steps on the path to healing. These people are angels. Know this. They will save you if you allow them in.

I tell it praying the lump in my throat will soften and the pain in my belly will subside.

I tell it, Goolrick concludes: "Because I do believe with all my heart that there is a persistence of song." Everyone knows how a song can make it all better. Sometimes, it's the only thing that can.

I tell it because I was called to be a mother, and I am humbled by the gift of motherhood.

I tell it as a reminder to put yourself first. We're no good to others if we're not physically and emotionally healthy.

And I tell it because I did what I thought was impossible: I couldn't change others, so I changed myself. I've entered that space where hope resides. Hope and faith sustain me.

Still, there are days when my soul is feeling bruised and orange. But with every new sunrise, I turn on the radio, find a favorite song and take it from the top.

ACKNOWLEDGEMENTS

This book owes its existence to many people. All those listed here made invaluable contributions. I offer them my heartfelt thanks.

Constance Costas, Contributing Editor

Joni Albrecht, Little Star Communications

Sam, Charlotte and Stuart

Robert

Barbara and Don Harrison

Tricia and Donny Harrison

The Book Club: Celeste, Lang, Ruthie and Sally

Pat Buxton

Marty Buxton

Kimberly Dowell-Spike

Elizabeth Cogar Batty

Judy Flohr

Lorna Wyckoff

Millie Cain

Ashley Farley

Beth Monroe

Carol Vig

Laurie and Gray Stettinius, Tuckahoe Creek Construction

Kip Dawkins, Photographer

Tasha Tolliver, Photographer

Martha Branch, Branch Marketing

The Frontier Press Team: Megan Herron, Cameron Huston, Erin Layne, Taylor Pilkington, and Katherine Schutt

Made in the USA
Columbia, SC
27 August 2017